-A

CW01648170

King Abdul-Aziz and the Kuwait Conference
1923–1924

In the name of God, the Merciful, the Compassionate

King Abdul-Aziz and the Kuwait Conference 1923–1924

Moudi Mansour Abdul-Aziz

Translated from the Arabic by
Basil Hatim with Ron Buckley

Echoes

British Library Cataloguing-in-Publication Data
A Catalogue record for this book is available from the British Library

ISBN 1 873395 79 5

First published 1993 by
Echoes
26 Westbourne Grove
London W2 5RH

© Moudi Mansour Abdul-Aziz 1993

Typeset by Group E, London

Contents

Acknowledgements

I should here like to acknowledge the much appreciated assistance extended to me by the Saudi Ministry of Foreign Affairs as represented by its various institutions, in addition to the valuable documents which the ministry placed at my disposal and which I used as important sources. I also wish to acknowledge the generous help of the House of King Abdul-Aziz in Riyadh with the *Najdi Green Book* (*al-Kitāb al-Akhdar*) and the basic statutes.

I should also like to take this opportunity to thank King Abdul-Aziz University in Mecca and its College of Shari'a and Islamic Studies. My thanks also go to my former supervisor, Dr Muhammad Abdul-Latif al-Bahrawi, Professor of Modern and Contemporary History and Islamic History at the College of Shari'a and Islamic Studies in Mecca, for his time and effort in preparing me to see this research through. I only hope that I have been successful in my attempts to study one aspect of this most important age of modern Arab and Islamic history, the age of Imam King Abdul-Aziz. My only remaining wish is that I have been able to make a new contribution to the literature on the subject.

Glossary

atawa	a tax
bādiya	desert
bid'a	unorthodox innovations in Islam
diyyat	blood money
fatwa	religious ruling
haj	pilgrimage
hajjana	camel corps
hijr (pl. *hijar*)	agricultural settlement
jihad	holy war
kharaj	land tax
khuwa	protection money
liwa'	military designation for a province within the Ottoman Empire
muhajirūn	those who emigrate; [by extension] inhabitants of *hijar*
mutassarif	Ottoman provincial governor
mutassarifiyya	administrative province within the Ottoman Empire
nawāhi	small administrative area within the Ottoman Empire
qā'imaqām	Ottoman administrative officer
qā'imaqamiyya	administrative district within the Ottoman Empire
qiyās	analogical reasoning
ulema	learned men of Islam
vilayet	largest administrative unit within the Ottoman Empire
wāli	Ottoman governor
waqf	state-administered religious endowment
zakat	alms tax (one of the five pillars of Islam)

Preface

My decision to work in the field of modern Islamic history was significantly influenced by my earlier studies of the various branches of modern history. More specifically, I was encouraged by the plans of the Modern History Department in Mecca to initiate a programme of research covering the Arabian peninsula in modern and contemporary times. I have thus chosen to write on the modern history of the peninsula, which could in fact be said to represent the history of the Saudi state in its three phases.

These three phases of the Saudi state resemble one another in many respects. The state is founded on the basis of the call for unity and reform, and on that of establishment and expansion. At the hands of His Majesty Imam King Abdul-Aziz, however, the third phase was to be particularly significant in the modern political and social spheres. The King had a unique talent in all these domains, which enabled him to be remarkably successful in establishing an Arab Islamic state on the principles of tradition and in harmony with the requirements of the modern age.

With this in mind, I decided to focus on a particular period during the era of Imam Abdul-Aziz, an era which he was to enrich and mark profoundly. When I embarked on some preliminary reading, I was impressed by the great deeds and achievements which this King—Abdul-Aziz bin Abdul-Rahman al-Feisal al-Saud—planned and brought about with enlightenment and vision. In this, he was guided by a sincere love for his homeland and an allegiance to his Arab and Islamic roots. I was struck by the extent of his knowledge and experience of every inch of this land, every well, every mountain, every valley, every tribe and every tribesman. Assisted only by the grace of God, and with no help from any outside power, he was ultimately able to give the peninsula both its independence and its unity.

During the course of my reading, I noticed that almost everything written about Imam King Abdul-Aziz was largely biographical, in works whose authors invariably pursued one particular line and simply adhered to a chronological sequence of events. The intellectual, political and economic achievements which characterized the age of this King, however, seemed to require a separate treatment of each of the issues, taking into account the age in its entirety. This motivated my choice of theme: King Abdul-Aziz and the Kuwait Conference, 1923–24.

In this endeavour, I was particularly encouraged by my success in gaining access to a collection of documents housed at the Public Record Office in London. These are from the Foreign Office archives, East Room (F.O. 371) and Long Room (F.O. 686). The documents include the correspondence, reports, bulletins and telegrams exchanged between the Foreign Office in London and its official representatives in several parts of the Arabian peninsula and the Gulf.

The outline of the book is as follows. Chapter 1 discusses the establishment of the Sultanate of Najd and its Dependencies. The regaining of Riyadh, al-Ihsā' and Hā'il and the annexation of 'Asīr are discussed in order to determine the boundaries of the new state; the alterations which these underwent in the process of the expansion of the state eastward, northward, westward and southward; and the consequences of all this for the border problems that should have been solved at the Kuwait Conference mentioned above.

Chapter 2, entitled *'Al-Ashrāf* and the First World War', deals with the contacts between Sherif Hussein and McMahon, the British High Commissioner in Egypt, and the extension of *al-Ashrāf* (i.e. the descendants of the Prophet Muhammad) rule to include Iraq and Transjordan under the mandate. This treatment aims to identify how the Saudi state was circumscribed and to describe King Abdul-Aziz's plan concerning this state of affairs prior to the Kuwait Conference.

Chapter 3 necessarily defines the relationship of the Sultanate of Najd with its neighbours, in the light of the positions adopted by the Ottoman Empire and Britain, and as an introduction to the preliminaries of the Kuwait Conference. Chapter 4 is devoted to a discussion of both the preliminaries and the three stages of the conference. Chapter 5 analyses and brings together the various strands which have emerged in the course of the work.

1
The Establishment of the Sultanate of Najd and its Dependencies

Regaining Riyadh, al-Ihsā' and Hā'il and the Annexation of 'Asīr

Any description of the establishment of the Sultanate of Najd and its Dependencies necessarily entails a discussion of the regaining of Riyadh and al-Ihsā', and the subjugation of Hā'il. The term 'regaining' is used advisedly here: in all his actions, King Abdul-Aziz was engaged in reclaiming only what had previously belonged to his ancestors. As we shall see when analysing this particular issue, the great state which King Abdul-Aziz took it upon himself to regain and establish underwent the same process and later expanded in the same way as that of the first Saudi state, with Riyadh being the foundation and point of departure. But the fact that the establishment of the new state was to start from Riyadh and spread eastward, northward and westward was in itself a source of problems; it had repercussions which were to form the basis on which relations were built between the state and forces both inside and outside the Arabian peninsula, as will become clearer in the following chapters.

However, since the discussion of the regaining of Riyadh and the annexation of al-Ihsā', Hā'il and other areas of the north is primarily intended to shed light on the history of the border problems and on other factors influencing the adjustment of relations, we shall not go into great detail regarding wars and strategies; these issues will be touched on only in so far as they have a direct bearing on the focus of this study.

The name 'Riyadh' first emerged when Dahham bin Dawwas bin Abdullah al-Sha'lan was its ruler. In this period, Riyadh became prominent at the expense of Hajr, which became a small part of the town and continued to lose importance until it ended up as merely the name of a well. In the eighteenth century, Riyadh was the name given to the orchards, gardens and rainwater pools round the town of Hajr.[1]

Rivalry between al-Dar'iyya and Riyadh started with the call of Sheikh Muhammad bin Abdul-Wahab and his permanent settlement in al-Dar'iyya, the oath of allegiance given to Imam Muhammad bin Saud, the establishment of the first Saudi state and the conversion of al-Dar'iyya into a base. This continued until Imam Turki bin Abdullah bin Muhammad bin Saud advanced towards Riyadh in 1824. From that time, Riyadh was the base of the Saudi state in its second phase.[2]

In the first year after Imam Abdullah bin Feisal bin Turki took control, he ordered the building of al-Musmak Palace, which took the place of the palace of Dahham bin Dawwas and the headquarters of his government. *Al-Musmak* means 'the lofty'. Others pronounce the word *al-Mismat* and interpret it as 'impregnable', or 'solidly shut' in the dialect of Najd.[3]

When, during the rule of Abdullah bin Feisal bin Turki, the sons of the Great Imam Muhammad bin Saud revolted against him, Muhammad bin Rashīd, the ruler of Hā'il, seized the opportunity and laid siege to Riyadh, entering it and appointing one of his men as governor together with Imam Abdul-Rahman bin Feisal bin Turki. Imam Abdul-Rahman, however, refused to acquiesce and consequently left for al-Ihsā', from where he attacked Riyadh, trying to recapture it. He finally retreated to al-Ihsā' in the face of desperate attempts on the part of Ibn Rashīd to maintain control. The *mutassarif* (provincial governor) of al-Ihsā' was 'Akif Pasha, who, on behalf of the Ottoman authorities, negotiated a deal with Imam Abdul-Rahman by which the Imam would become Emir of Riyadh in return for recognizing the authority of the Sublime Porte and paying a sum of money. But Imam Abdul-Rahman refused to succumb to any outside pressure. In fact, he had had a deep-seated hatred of foreign powers ever since Muhammad Ali's subversive activities in Najd. (When barely 8 years of age, Imam Abdul-Rahman's son, Imam Abdul-Aziz, had witnessed these developments.) Riyadh subsequently became a dependency of the Emirate of Hā'il from 1891 to 1901.[4]

Imam Abdul-Rahman left his homeland for Kuwait. With him was his son Abdul-Aziz who, like all the youth of the Al Saud, had been raised on the principles of religion and valour. In Kuwait, young Abdul-Aziz continued to be preoccupied with the land he had left behind.

At the same time, Abdul-Aziz bin Mit'ib bin Rashīd, the Emir of the

Jabal who usurped Najd, continued his raids on Kuwait, hoping to devour it too. Sheikh Mubarak, the ruler of Kuwait, appealed to the Ottomans for help and subsequently entered into an alliance with Imam Abdul-Rahman to form a united front against Abdul-Aziz bin Mit'ib bin Rashīd. In 1901 the two sides engaged in battle midway between Kuwait, Hā'il and Buraida: Imam Abdul-Rahman al-Feisal and Sheikh Mubarak's men, on one side, and the men of the Emir of the Jabal in al-Suraif, on the other. The battle ended in favour of the Emir of the Jabal, who was made over-confident by his victory and decided to march on Kuwait. At this point, we may wonder what would have happened had the troops coming from Kuwait won. The answer is that Najd could probably have been regained. But this immediately raises another question: what would have happened had Ibn Rashīd been able to occupy Kuwait? The answer is that the course of history would certainly have been altered. However, Ibn Rashīd was forced to forsake Kuwait and retreat.[5]

As the campaign launched by Imam Abdul-Rahman and the Sheikh of Kuwait covered the al-Summan and al-Dahna' areas and reached Wādī al-Shawki, Prince Abdul-Aziz bin Abdul-Rahman asked his father for permission to head directly for Riyadh. Permission was granted, and Abdul-Aziz surprised the towns and villages *en route*, reached Riyadh and entered it. The Emir of Riyadh at that time was one of the Rashīd family, 'Ajlan bin Muhammad. But when Abdul-Aziz received the news of the fall of al-Suraif, he immediately left Riyadh and returned to Kuwait.

Although Abdul-Aziz had to withdraw from Riyadh, this particular event was a useful lesson which helped him to reassess, and gave him first-hand experience of, the strength of the city from which he had been absent for ten years. He greatly benefited from the four months he spent in Riyadh inspecting its various areas, roads, walls and other fortifications.[6]

In 1901, and in total secrecy, Abdul-Aziz left Kuwait accompanied by forty men from the Al Saud and others loyal to it, and about twenty of their followers. Although historians differ as to exactly how many accompanied Abdul-Aziz, there is general agreement that they were around sixty men, whose names are inscribed in the annals of the modern history of the Arabian peninsula. These names were probably the ones actually inscribed on a plaque in the House of King Abdul-Aziz in Riyadh.[7]

Riyadh was Abdul-Aziz's target. It was the power base of his forefathers. It was also sufficiently distant from the power base of Ibn Rashīd, who resided in Hā'il. Finally, the people of Riyadh and southern Najd were particularly loyal to the Al Saud. Abdul-Aziz and his company took up quarters at a place two hours from Riyadh known as Dail 'Ushub. He then arrived at the house of a man from Najd next to al-Musmak Palace belonging to ʻAjlan. That was the day of the battle of al-Musmak and the regaining of Riyadh. The news travelled rapidly throughout the Arabian peninsula.[8] When Ibn Rashīd learned that Abdul-Aziz was in the country, he invaded Kuwait, and at the same time entered into negotiations with the Ottoman *wāli* (governor) in Baghdad, hoping that he would eventually be able to occupy Kuwait, and then regain Riyadh with the help of the Ottoman garrison in al-Ihsāʼ.

The day after the situation stabilized in Riyadh, Abdul-Aziz left for the south, heading towards al-Kharj, al-Huta, al-Hariq, al-Aflaj and al-Dawasir. He was able to consolidate his position on a triangular front, with al-ʻArid at the top, and with a base that extended along the northern borders up to the Empty Quarter, from Yibrin to Wādī al-Dawasir. This is how Ibn Rashīd lost Riyadh and with it the wide base in the south, his attention being divided between invading Kuwait and capturing Riyadh, in neither of which he was successful.[9]

The subsequent fall of ʻUnaiza and Buraida was particularly significant. After taking control of the whole of Najd, Abdul-Aziz came to threaten the entire surrounding area. The battles of ʻUnaiza, Buraida, al-Bakiriyya, al-Shanana and al-Rus, which commenced at the beginning of 1904, were all battles to regain al-Qasīm. It was in the battle of al-Bakiriyya, however, that Ottoman involvement became more apparent. Realizing that Abdul-Aziz would not be satisfied with regaining Najd alone, the Ottomans were supplying ammunition and men to fight alongside Ibn Rashīd.[10]

But the situation did not develop in favour of the Ottomans, who were preoccupied with the revolt of Imam Yahya in Yemen and his siege of Sanʻāʼ. This forced them to recall some of their generals from the above-mentioned front and send them to Yemen instead.[11]

The battle of Rawdat Muhana in 1906 was decisive, resulting in the death of the Emir of Hāʼil; he was succeeded by his son, Mitʻib bin Abdul-Aziz bin Mitʻib al-Rashīd. The latter yearned for peace and stability and thus entered into negotiations which led to Hāʼil and its dependencies together with Shammar coming under his control, while Najd, including al-Qasīm, went to Abdul-Aziz.[12]

This meant the annexation of al-Qasīm, which completed the process of regaining the whole of Najd, including its middle, southern and northern parts. At the same time, this was an indication that the Al Saud were holding sway and becoming the greatest power in the Arabian peninsula. It was also a sign of future developments in the peninsula in general. Because of the changes in the heart of the peninsula, the Sheikh of Kuwait no longer faced the spectre of danger from the Rashīd family, or at least saw that danger as reduced. He was nevertheless worried by the victories which Abdul-Aziz was achieving. He thus sought to attain a balance of power in the north of the peninsula, a desire which became obvious in the battle of Tarafiyya, or al-Ahzāb, north of Buraida, which took place on 14 December 1907.

Al-Ihsā' used to be a part of the area once referred to as Bahrain or Hajr, extending from the frontiers of Basra to the coasts of Oman. It had the name Ihsā', or al-Hasa, as it had numerous water courses just under the surface. Al-Hufūf, which used to be called Hajr, is its best-known town. After the fourth century AH this came to be known as al-Hasa, a name which was then used to refer to the whole area. Al-'Uqair, on the other hand, was a market town in the Arabian peninsula and an important trade centre overlooking the waters of the Gulf. Imports from India arrived here first and were then exported to the north of the peninsula. The entire coast of al-Hasa was called al-Khat.[13]

Al-Hasa came to be dominated by the tribe of Banu Khalid, a fact which aroused the envy of Banu Muntafik, which had the biggest influence in the desert of southern Iraq. The Ottomans used to refer to both al-Ihsā' and al-Qatīf as Najd *liwa'* (province), which was administered by a *mutassarif* who took his orders directly from the Basra administration. Chaos reigned in this area, keeping the *mutassarif*, his garrison and his staff behind the walls of the city, and leaving the roads to the bedouin to rob and generally abuse travellers. The 'Ajman dominated al-Ihsā', and Banu Hajir and Banu Khalid dominated al-Qatīf, while Banu Murra, the Manasīr and some of Banu Hajir dominated the caravan routes.[14]

A document in the form of telegram no. 222677 from General Sidqī Pasha of the Sultan's Sixth Army in Baghdad contained a response to the Sultan's decree that regular troops be sent to the *liwa'* of Najd in order to restore law and order. The telegram stated that security in the province had deteriorated so badly that people who supported Prince Abdul-Aziz had written secretly to inform Sidqī Pasha that if he wanted to take full control of the province, he would be received in the city[15] with open arms. The document also mentioned that Abdul-Aziz was fighting Ibn Rashīd in al-Qasīm province and that it would be difficult for the local government to defend al-Ihsā' in the event of an attack by Abdul-Aziz.[16]

Another telegram, no. 209859, from Major-General Sulaiman Pasha of the Sultan's Sixth Army in Baghdad, mentioned that the people of Najd and the tribes of its desert were suffering. They were enduring much greater hardship than the people of any other *liwa'* in the Ottoman Empire, and it was the duty of everyone and in the general interest to redouble efforts in order to win their approval by easing their tyrannical treatment at the hands of state officials. These officials had been doing everything to upset the indigenous population, creating considerable resentment. The people had taken up arms, raised their flags in rebellion, and closed down their shops in the town and in the surrounding villages.[17]

The Office of the Grand Vizier also received a telegram from the *wāli* and the Commander of Basra stating that the local government had announced a price for dates in the centre of Najd *liwa'* which some people considered to have exceeded the previous price. This proved damaging to the people of the area and thus led to anti-government sentiment. There was also talk that the *mutassarif* of Najd and its Commander were complaining about each other and that the relationship between them was far from harmonious.[18] Similar sentiments were expressed regarding the administrative district of Najd and the *liwa'* of Najd in another document from the papers of the Sublime Porte, Diwan-i Hamayun, no. 2684, deposited in the Cabinet archives in Istanbul.

In 1911 the Italians attacked Tripoli. No sooner had this Italian–Turkish war ended than the first Balkan war started in 1912. At the same time, conflict among the Rashīd family in Hā'il erupted. These circumstances were sufficient reason to make an attack on al-Hasa most opportune. The Ottomans had already started to incite the Mutair and 'Ajman tribes from al-Hasa against Imam Abdul-Aziz.

In addition to the revenue generated from al-Ihsā', this city offered the only access from Najd to the Arabian Gulf and beyond. This is why Abdul-Aziz yearned for the day when he could regain al-Hasa. That day came in 1913. Abdul-Aziz took advantage of the weakness of the Ottoman Empire in the aftermath of its war with the Italians and the Balkan wars, and the withdrawal of part of its garrison from al-Hufūf.[19] This was made clear by Imam Abdul-Aziz in an interview with an Iraqi reporter, in which the Imam said:

> The High State [the Ottoman Empire] usurped this province from my forefathers. I only wish they had occupied countries in the lower parts of al-Ihsā', such as Oman, etc., instead of neglecting them, thus enabling foreign countries to plant the seeds of division among their people and thereby achieve what they were after. Ever since, things have been deteriorating for the people of this province, who have fallen victim to brigands. They complained to the higher authorities but to no avail. I have received petitions signed by many *ulema* [learned men of Islam] and dignitaries, on which I relied finally in seeking what is mine by right in this province.[20]

Thus, there were sufficient reasons for Imam Abdul-Aziz to seek access to the sea lest he should one day find himself besieged in the midst of the desert. The Arabian Gulf was the nearest point for him to achieve this aim.

Many historians regard the fall of al-Musmak fortress as the first decisive strike, and the battle of Rawdat Muhana as the second. The third was the fall of the town of al-Hufūf.[21] Led by Imam Abdul-Aziz, the Saudi soldiers advanced into al-Ihsā' province until they reached one of its wells, 1.6 kilometres from al-Hufūf. At that time, the Ottomans had four fortresses in al-Ihsā': three of them were in al-Hufūf itself, and one was in the town of al-Mibraz, 2 kilometres from al-Hufūf.[22]

Al-Hufūf was the largest city in the Eastern Province. It was divided into two sectors. The western sector, called al-Kūt, was fortified by walls and covered nearly half of the town, including government offices, the residences of the Turkish families and Ibrahim Palace, which was more strongly fortified than al-Musmak fortress in Riyadh. The eastern sector, on the other hand, was not fortified; it was inhabited by the people of al-Ihsā' and was the site of the commercial markets. Surrounding al-Kūt were walls, towers and a trench. Within these walls thousands of Turkish officers and soldiers were gathered, fully armed with small arms and cannon.

The Imam addressed his men, informing them of his intention to attack al-Kūt. He planned for his soldiers to infiltrate the walls at night, instructing them to move in quietly. When they reached al-Kūt, they began tying tree trunks together, making a ladder which ten of them climbed. Others began to demolish part of the wall, creating a gap through which Abdul-Aziz and those who accompanied him entered. The *mutassarif* of al-Hufūf and the Commander of its garrison were eventually forced to surrender. Following this, the garrison departed to al-'Uqair and then to Bahrain, although they were not allowed to take their cannon and ammunition, which stayed inside the fortresses.[23] The Imam later sent a battalion of his soldiers led by Abdul-Rahman bin Sweilim to al-Qatīf, whose people immediately surrendered; those who had been manning the garrison fled by ship to Bahrain.

The Ottomans did not object to the new *status quo*. The First World War was looming on the horizon. They thus tried through diplomatic means to solve a problem which had proved militarily insurmountable. A delegation headed by Tālib al-Naqīb was sent to talk to the Imam, who attended the meeting held at al-Sabiha near Kuwait.[24] The Ottoman authorities asked to be allowed accredited representatives in al-Qatīf and al-Ihsā', a request which the Imam refused. Eventually, the *wāli* of Basra received a telegram informing him of the recognition of the Imam as *wāli* of Najd and of al-Ihsā'. This recognition extended not only to him, but to his sons, his grandsons and any of his other descendants. The Imam was also granted the rank of Pasha. Thus instead of punishing him, the Ottomans were now forced to try to win him over.[25]

We are thus inclined to disagree with the author of *Ma'a 'Ahil al-Jazīra al-'Arabiyya*, who argues that the reason for invading al-Hasa was that the policy of the Ottoman Empire was basically to play off the Sultan of Najd against the Sherif of Mecca, an aim which Ibn Saud realized by seizing al-Hasa.[26]

As Britain had a vested interest in the route to India via the Arabian Gulf, the Saudi advance on al-Ihsā' was seen to lead to an imbalance of power on the Gulf coast. A number of British Foreign Office documents in the Public Record Office testify to Britain's plans to thwart the Ottoman domination of the coastal areas east of the Arabian peninsula and indicate the means adopted by Britain to undermine Ottoman sovereignty in the area. Searching ships alleged to be engaged in piracy was one of these means.[27]

In the light of the Ottomans' acceptance of Imam Abdul-Aziz's annexation of al-Ihsā', and given their attempt to win him over instead of punishing him, Britain saw fit to opt for neutrality. Sheikh Mubarak, the Emir of Kuwait, had a part to play in all this, but it amounted to no more than sounding out Britain as to what its position really was.[28]

Britain later resorted to quiet diplomacy. It sent Captain Shakespear, its Political Agent in Kuwait, to Riyadh, deputizing for Sir Percy Cox, the British Political Resident in the Gulf. Cox[29] arrived after British troops had occupied Basra in Iraq. Britain's interests in India were increasingly involved.

On direct instructions from London, the British authorities in India became more interested in contacting Imam Abdul-Aziz who, by taking al-Hasa, now had access to the Arabian Gulf. These contacts were intended to relay Britain's desire to become friendly with the new state in the Arabian peninsula and to express its appreciation of the ability of this state to prevent the various tribes from lapsing into their old ways and to promote justice, law and order.[30]

Thus the expansion of Imam Abdul-Aziz's state to the north and the north-west created relations and problems peculiar to the region and to the Ottoman Empire. The eastward expansion of the state, on the other hand, increased the importance of its relationship with both the Ottoman Empire and Britain. This was helped by the start of the First World War and by the need of both the Ottomans and the British to woo this emerging regional power.[31]

We should always bear in mind, however, the virtues which characterized the new state, and which were admired by friend and foe alike. These virtues emanated from adherence to tradition, an adherence to which its founder's forebears had subscribed and which allowed the new state to control the various tribes and promote law and order. It was this very image which was later to expose the corruption of other regimes alien to the nature of Arabian peninsular society.

The contacts conducted so far were to be the prelude to the Qatīf treaty,[32] concluded with Britain in 1915. Similarly, the Qatīf treaty was a prelude to the trust and respect which Britain was obliged to extend to this new state.[33] Imam Abdul-Aziz was a man of extraordinary qualities, and it soon became clear that he was the only person capable of ensuring the peninsula's independence, security and prosperity. From its past experience with the Saudi state under the Great Imam Saud, the British Government of India was aware of the importance of friendly relations with the new state.[34] The Qatīf treaty was the last to be modelled on the kind of treaties which Britain had concluded with the Gulf states. However, the treaty was particularly beneficial to Imam Abdul-Aziz: it involved Britain's recognition of his annexation of al-Ihsā', al-Qatīf, al-Jubail and the entire coastal area; it also gave him the opportunity to discipline the 'Ajman tribes.[35]

Jabal Shammar province is considered to be the northern part of Najd. The Jabal used to be called Jabal Te' Aja' wa Salma, extending from the south-west to the north-east, with a plain between that is full of fertile valleys of orchards and farms, among which stands Hā'il.[36] Hā'il is the best known of the cities in this area. It takes its name from the fact that it is situated between Najd and its northern Dependencies. As for Jabal Shammar, the name goes back to the Shammar tribe, who are the descendants of Qahtāni Arabs.[37]

The traveller Carsten Niebuhr, considered to be the first Westerner to speak about Najd, says that it extends from al-Ihsā' and Iraq to Hejaz, and from Najrān and Qahtān or Yemen to the desert of al-Shām. Niebuhr goes on to say that also part of Najd is the mountain area known as al-Jof al-Sarhan, which is situated between Jabal Shammar and al-Shām and which includes Sakaka and Doma, referred to by Abu al-Fida as Domat al-Jandal. In his classification of Najd, Niebuhr considers both Jabal Shammar, with Hā'il as its base, and al-Jof in the extreme north to be parts of Najd.[38]

As mentioned above, Hā'il used to be part of Najd. It was governed on behalf of the Al Saud by the Rashīd family, who took advantage of the fragmentation of the Saudi state and besieged Riyadh. While still in his youth, Imam Abdul-Aziz bin Abdul-Rahman took part in one of the negotiating sessions between the two parties.[39] All this gave the Imam sufficient reason to set his sights on Hā'il, the key to which was the subjugation of al-Qasīm.

The Ottomans tried to preserve the Emirate of the Rashīd family in Hā'il, so as to curb the power of Imam Abdul-Aziz and prevent him becoming a threat to the Ottoman presence in the peninsula as a whole.

Thus, when Abdul-Aziz bin Mit'ib bin Abdullah bin Ali bin Rashīd (who had ruled Hā'il in 1896) fled to al-Kahfa, one of the villages of Hā'il, after the battle of al-Shanana in 1904 and requested help from the Ottomans once more, they responded favourably. They sent Field Marshal Ahmad Faidi Pasha, who arrived from Baghdad with three battalions and five artillery units under his command, and Lieutenant-General Sidqī Pasha, who arrived from al-Madīnāh with two battalions under his command. The two contingents met and camped near al-Qasīm. The Ottomans proposed that al-Qasīm be turned into a buffer zone between Ibn Saud and the Rashīd family where a military command centre could be set up and a number of military advisers stationed. These wishes, however, were all flatly rejected.[40]

When Saud bin Abdul-Aziz bin Mit'ib bin Abdullah bin Ali bin Rashīd took over and occupied al-Jof at the instigation of Sherif Hussein of Mecca, who supplied him with money and arms,[41] Imam Abdul-Aziz was awaiting his chance to put an end to the reign of the Rashīd family in Hā'il and settle old scores with them. A number of factors later created this opportunity, including: Britain's preoccupation with the Arab revolts which continued in Iraq, al-Shām (i.e. Greater Syria) and Palestine; the differences within the Rashīd family; and the improvement of Saudi–Kuwaiti relations. But the most important factor which helped the Imam was the spread of his call for unity and reform among the Shammar tribes. Thus, he was able to advance towards Hā'il, which he besieged until it fell in November 1921. Al-Qasīm was the base from which these operations were mounted. Muhammad bin Talal bin Rashīd and other dignitaries surrendered and the rule of the Rashīd family came to an end after nearly ninety-one years.[42]

The subjugation of the Jabal opened the road to the north and the north-west. Immediately after the capture of Hā'il, al-Jof, which is ideally situated on the caravan route between Najd and al-Shām,[43] opted to join the Saudi state. The Saudi soldiers continued their advance to Khaibar.

It is said that the Jof country, including most importantly Sakaka and Domat al-Jandal, was once a sea lower than Wādī al-Sarhan. Al-Jof is characterized by an abundance of wells and orchards, with every oasis consisting of a well and an orchard surrounded by a wall. Al-Jof had a palace built by Mit'ib bin Abdullah bin Ali bin Rashīd, which the Rashīdi rulers of al-Jof used regularly. There was a small group of soldiers to protect the palace and police the area. Previously, al-Jof had been only a fiefdom of the Sha'lan family, the Sheikhs of the Emirate of the Rashīd family. But Mit'ib bin Rashīd put an end to this and the area has ever since been considered a part of Najd. The inhabitants of al-Jof are a mixture of tribes from the area, including al-Rola, al-'Amarat, al-Huwaita, the 'Anza, the Mawahib and the Shammar. Sakaka is some 32 kilometres from al-Jof.[44]

The small town of Qaf, on the other hand, was one of the villages of al-Milh. It was subjected to attacks launched on Wādī al-Sarhan from Damascus, but its inhabitants always felt that they belonged to the Jabal, and thus used to pay *atawa* (a tax) to the deputies of Ibn Rashīd. Only two and a half hours to the east was a richer village in Wādī al-Sarhan. It exported salt, mostly to Busra in the north. It is possible that Wādī al-Sarhan was once entirely a lake like the Dead Sea; it is 20 kilometres wide, contains numerous wells and has water close to the surface for the irrigation of palm groves. It also had a large salt-water lake which had dried up with time and was subsequently used to collect salt, which the caravans carried away. Tamarind trees, which are a source of wood, were plentiful. The place was also known as Tammorat al-Hilwa. Seasonal rains were sometimes late, forcing the tribes to desert the valley. Brigandage was rife.[45]

Yet Wādī al-Sarhan enjoyed an important strategic position, militarily, economically and commercially. It is on the trade route which links the heart of the Arabian peninsula to al-Shām, covering particularly the Red Sea coastal area. For a very long time, it had been inhabited by the Rola tribe, which had latterly been headed by the Sha'lan family, who used to live in Damascus and were thus inclined to accept the notion of annexation to Syria. In fact, Wādī al-Sarhan was originally known as Wādī al-Azraq. It acquired the new name after the Sarhan tribe migrated from Horan and settled here nearly two centuries before. But it is this which explains the wish of those outside the Arabian peninsula to acquire the wādī and its two main towns, al-Jof and Sakaka. It was also this which led Imam Abdul-Aziz to believe that the occupation of the wādī was inevitable, particularly as it would provide him with a gap through which he could gain direct access to Syria. Thus, the first step was to send people who preached the fundamentalist Salafi call there,[46] followed by its annexation. When discussing the Kuwait Conference, we shall see how the delegation of Transjordan insisted on the withdrawal of Imam Abdul-Aziz from the wādī, while the delegation of Najd maintained that it was an integral part of the Jabal, i.e. of Najd.

Next was 'Asīr, divided into a coastal plain called Tihamat 'Asīr and a mountainous area called 'Asīr al-Sirrat. In the Ottoman era, until 1912, the 'Asīr *liwa'* was bordered by Sa'da to the south and Zahran to the north. On the Tihama front, it was bordered by Wādī Abi 'Arish to the south and Wādī Doqa near al-Laith to the north. To the east were Qahtān tribes east of Sa'da, to the north-east Wādī Bisha, and to the west the Red Sea. 'Asīr is the tribe which gave its name to the area: Bilad 'Asīr or Dirat 'Asīr.[47]

The people of 'Asīr are Shafi'is and fundamentalist (Salafi) Hanbalites. In the days of the earlier Al Saud rulers, the people of 'Asīr wholeheartedly accepted the call of Sheikh Muhammad bin Abdul-Wahab and paid their *zakat* (alms tax) to the Imam at al-Dar'iyya. Ali bin Mihthal became 'Asīr's Emir and a follower of al-Dar'iyya. When he was attacked by the armies of Muhammad Ali, Ali bin Mihthal defended 'Asīr, assisted by 'Ayid bin Mar'i, whom he nominated as his successor. When al-Dar'iyya fell, 'Ayid bin Mar'i declared independence there and was succeeded by his son Muhammad, who extended the Emirate eastward to Bisha, northward to the Hejaz borders and southward to Mecca in Tihama. The Ottoman authorities sent him Field Marshal Radif Pasha to lead a campaign which turned 'Asīr into a *mutassarifiyya* (administrative province) whose centre of government was Abha. Muhammad bin 'Ayid was killed, but his successors remained as assistants to the Ottoman *mutassarif* of 'Asīr.[48]

In the period which followed the promulgation of the constitution, the Ottoman Empire was preoccupied with troubles of its own. There was, for example, the uprising of Muhammad Ali al-Idrisi (1911), who exercised his influence on Tihama from the north of al-Hudaida to the south of Qunfuda and part of Jabal al-Surat. He bought arms from Italy and had them shipped to him in Italian vessels. He also brought under his control the area between Sabya and Abha. The *mutassarif* of Abha, Sulaiman Shafiq Kamali Pasha, was unable to put up any resistance and was besieged in the town. When the Ottoman Turks were thus besieged in Abha by Muhammad Ali al-Idrisi, with nowhere to turn to and fearful of the rebellion of the 'Ayid family, the *mutassarif* extended the hand of friendship and made them partners in the running of the country. He appointed Hasan bin Ali bin Muhammad bin 'Ayid as his assistant and Abha was liberated. Sulaiman Shafiq Kamali Pasha left for Iraq and was succeeded by Muhi al-Din Pasha, Hasan remaining an assistant. The Ottoman flag continued to fly over the hills of 'Asīr until the First World War.[49] At the end of the war, the Ottomans withdrew from 'Asīr and Hasan bin Ali bin Muhammad bin 'Ayid declared independence. Ibn 'Ayid was an autocrat and this aroused the resentment of the inhabitants, who consequently complained about him to Imam Abdul-Aziz.

The above sequence of events helps to explain why the 'Asīris did not seek help from Sherif Hussein in Hejaz or from the Imam of Yemen, both of whom were geographically closer to them than Najd. Was it because Imam Abdul-Aziz was the strongest? The answer is that the 'Asīris felt that the founder of their emirate, 'Ayid al-Yazid, was a dependant of the ruler of Najd, paying him *kharaj* (land tax) and *zakat*. He and almost all of the 'Asīris were believers in Salafiyya, an allegiance which the people of 'Asīr have inherited ever since.

Imam Abdul-Aziz nominated a delegation of *ulema* to go to the Emir of Abha. The delegation, however, was not well received by the Emir. As a consequence, Imam Abdul-Aziz decided to send a force led by his cousin,

Abdul-Aziz bin Musa'id bin Jalawi, in 1921. Hasan bin 'Ayid tried to seek help from Sherif Hussein, who supplied him with funds and arms. But Hasan bin 'Ayid finally succumbed. In another campaign led by Emir Feisal in 1923, the 'Ayid Emirate was finally crushed.[50]

The foregoing makes it clear that the state which was established prior to the Kuwait Conference by Imam Abdul-Aziz began in Najd (1902–08) and then extended to al-Ihsā' (1913).

In the summer of 1921 a conference was held in Riyadh, attended by the Emirs, *ulema* and other dignitaries of the land. After deliberations concerning the current situation in and the future of Najd, as well as the method of governing it, it was decided that the title Sultan of Najd be bestowed on Imam Abdul-Aziz. Hā'il was annexed in 1921, and then 'Asīr in 1922. The Sultanate of Najd and its Dependencies was thus established.[51]

Border Disputes

Parallel to the gradual establishment of the Sultanate of Najd and its Dependencies along the lines described above, border disputes began to arise, concentrated in the north and west. These can be divided into two types. The first concerns the fact that these areas were inhabited by nomadic tribes who had for centuries grazed their livestock unrestricted by political borders. The entire area was part of the Ottoman Empire. But the historical developments which led to the establishment of two new states occupying the borders of the Sultanate of Najd and its [northern] Dependencies, in addition to Hejaz in the west, created a new situation which accentuated these border problems. In fact, some of the tribes were divided into two parts, one in the Sultanate of Najd and the other in one of the neighbouring states, either in the north or in the west.

The second kind of problem emerged as a result of strategic conditions, as pointed out earlier. These include, for example, the importance of Wādī al-Sarhan with its two main towns, al-Jof and Sakaka, and its strategic importance to Syria and Transjordan while still remaining an integral part of the Sultanate of Najd and its Dependencies.

Ecologists, who study the relationship between living organisms and their environment, consider the area of the northern borders of the Sultanate of Najd to offer a model of bedouin society. Ecology explains the extent to which the natural habitat of the bedouin is related to factors such as rain, temperature, groundwater, animals, grazing land and grassland. This science also demonstrates that, in this area, the human factor is bound up with the natural environment. Within this perspective, the areas which emerge are

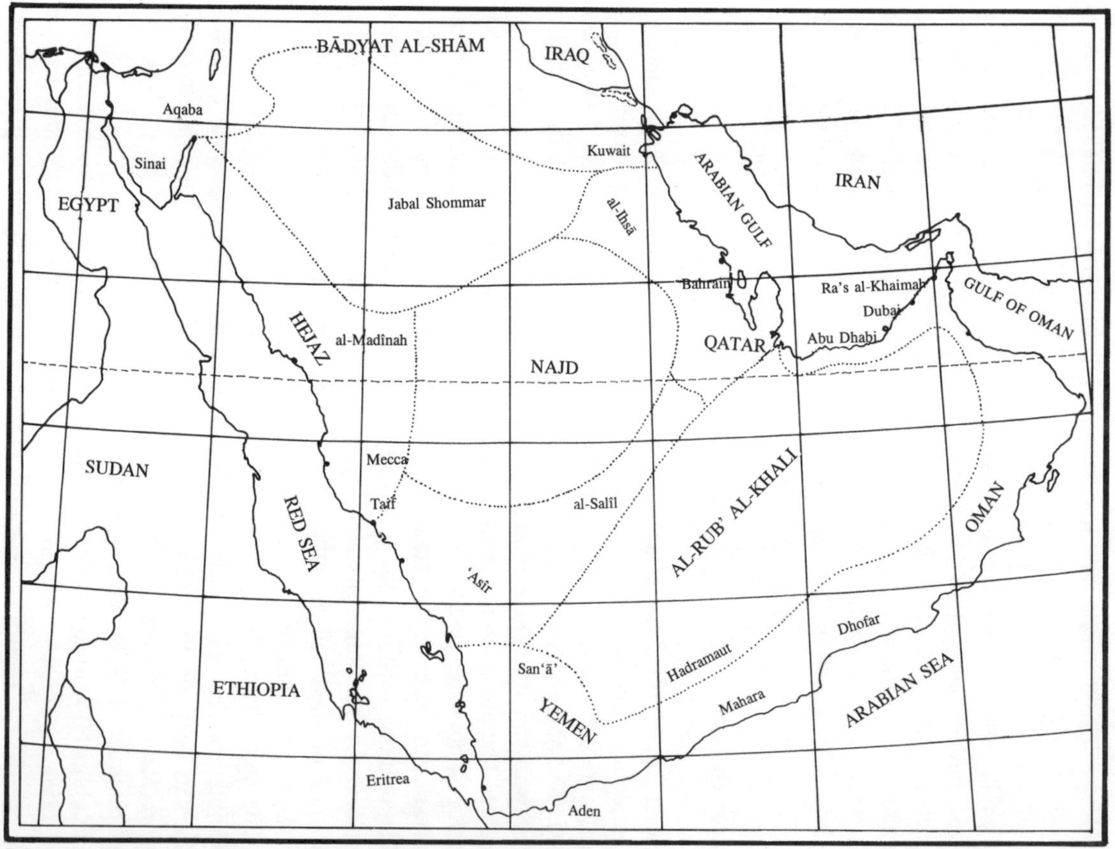

Map I. Najd, al-Ihsā', Jabal Shammar and 'Asīr

called 'the margin of the north'. This points to the fact that the conditions of extreme dryness and scarcity of grazing land have created the need to move from one place to another. It also demonstrates that bedouin life increased in the northern border region, consequently leading to an increase in dispersal and mobility.[52]

To illustrate this tribal intermeshing, we may cite the example of Banu Harb, who had one section in Najd and the other in Hejaz; hence we have the Najdi Harb and the Hejazi Harb. Another example is the Huwaitat, who were scattered between Taima' in the south, al-Karak in the north, Wādī al-Sarhan and al-Nufud al-Kabir in the east and the Gulf of Aqaba and the Sinai peninsula in the west. The Manazil al-Thafir were divided between Najd and Iraq and the surrounding areas. The Shammar were located west of al-Qasīm. The Mutair extended from the Kuwait border to the area near al-Qasīm.[53] This tribe was known as the 'Najdi Knights' and also as 'Those who Return', a reference to their valour: no matter how much of a beating they took in battle, they were always able to make a come-back and defeat their enemies.

The Huwaitat tribes, for example, and particularly one sub-tribe called the Tawabha, used to launch attacks from Ma'n on the Najdi–Hejazi tribes. They were constantly on the move between Wajh al-Hejaz, Tabuk and Tihamat al-Wajh, some of them entering Jordan from Hasma' and Yakhim on the Rum front. Tribal clashes were also common on the Saudi–Iraqi borders. Some of these skirmishes resulted in Najdi tribes being able to reach the area just outside Najaf and Karbala' inside Iraqi territory, occasionally being rebuffed by British tanks and planes.

The raids of the Zain tribes on the people of Najd are fairly well documented. The Zain are a sub-group of Banu Sakhr, who were originally part of Banu Harb. According to the statement submitted to the Kuwait Conference, the loot in these raids amounted to 1,040 camels and merchandise estimated to be worth 80,000 Turkish Liras.[54]

Thus, any negotiations concerning the border problems were held up by numerous stumbling-blocks, including the fact that the bedouin knew no borders. Nor was there a mountain or a river which could be taken as a clear demarcation line. Finally, disputes always arose regarding whom a particular tribe belonged to.[55]

Lady Anne Blunt, in her book *A Pilgrimage to Nejd*,[56] describes a journey she made to the area. When she asked a guide how he made his living, she was told that raiding was his profession and that he was one of a group of nine from Shammar in Horan who went out together to al-Zarqa' or to al-Lajāt al-Gharbiyya, stealing livestock. He also told her how one day they were subjected to an attack from the Rola.

At a General Assembly in Najd in 1928, speakers addressed Imam Sultan Abdul-Aziz, telling him that:

> The entire *bādiya* [desert] is ours, we the people of Najd. We therefore register our protest about your unjust decision to contain us within borders in this *bādiya*. You then responded that border demarcation does not mean giving up the possession of land, but is only a way of settling disputes which might arise in the *bādiya*. You also told us that we were free to graze anywhere we liked in this *bādiya*.[57]

After the annexation of al-Qasīm, the Imam was thus forced to fight the Mutair and bring them under his control, though their chieftain Feisal al-Dawish managed to escape. The Imam then appointed his cousin Emir Abdullah bin Jalawi al-Saud as Emir of al-Qasīm, to punish those tribes which violated law and order.

The 'Ajman, on the other hand, were originally tribes from Najrān who migrated north-eastward, reaching al-Ihsā' in the era of Imam Turki bin Abdullah. The Imam received them well and allowed them to settle in the Banu Khalid area, but they were troublesome, constantly causing problems and often molesting travellers and pilgrim caravans. The harm they caused extended beyond al-Ihsā' and included Kuwait, whose Emir asked Imam Abdul-Aziz to punish them and to return what they had looted. The Imam went after them in the summer of 1915. In that scorching summer, a horrific battle took place near Kansan. The Imam was forced to return to al-Hufūf, followed by the 'Ajman, who besieged the town.[58]

Prior to that, in January 1915, the 'Ajman had retreated in the battle of Jarāb between Imam Abdul-Aziz and Ibn Rashīd. At the same time, the Mutair attacked and sacked the camp of the Emir of Hā'il. Both the Saudi and the Rashīdi commanders were preoccupied with pursuing the looters and the battle was indecisive.[59] The 'Ajman fled to the British protectorate of Kuwait and the Imam had to enter into negotiations with Sir Percy Cox, the British Political Resident in the Gulf.

The Muntafik tribes were similarly part of these border problems. The Sa'dun family, leaders of al-Muntafik, were the dominant force in the area in the days of the Ottoman Empire. When the British occupied Iraq, they struck at the Sa'dun family's sphere of influence and promoted the second tier of tribal chieftains, using them to supply the British forces with livestock and provisions, and as support against the Sa'dun family.[60] The obstinacy of al-Muntafik in Iraq was such that they threatened Kuwait, and defeated Sheikh Mubarak's army in more than one battle, thus forcing the Sheikh to double the tax on pearl-traders.[61]

It was with such developments in mind that Imam Sultan Abdul-Aziz issued orders to all the Najdi tribes and clans that acts of aggression against neighbours were banned, that the flag of raiding could be flown only with his consent and that anyone flouting these decrees would be punished by death and the confiscation of his assets.[62]

After the circle widened with the establishment of the Emirate of Transjordan and the Kingdom of Iraq, it became obvious that this policy of encirclement was helped by two crucial factors. The first concerned the Shammar tribes, who, after Hā'il was retaken, sought refuge in Iraq and began to launch attacks on Najd. The second factor concerned the Rola tribes, who took orders from Ibn Sha'lan and acted in concert with Emir Abdullah of Transjordan, with the aim of embarking on acts of aggression intended to help the Jordanians extend their power base to include al-Jof.[63]

The 'Anza tribe, whose men were renowned for their horsemanship, may be traced back to Wa'il bin Rabi'a. The tribe had three major groups. One, called Banu Wahab, was divided into two sub-groups. The first of these, called Wulid Ali, settled in al-Shām *bādiya* between al-Balqa' and Horan. Their pattern of movement ran as follows: in cold and snowy weather, they would stock up with the necessary grain and, with their camels, horses and other livestock, head for an area of Dūmmat al-Jandal wa al-Shām called Wādī al-Sarhan and al-Hammad; in summer, they would return to their customary homes. These two sub-groups of Banu Wahab had allowances and *kharaj* which were given to tribal chieftains for protecting the roads and the farmlands from their own people and for preventing raids and attacks on Aleppo and Damascus by the other 'Anza tribes which were settled in Najd.

Another group within the 'Anza was called al-Rola. They were the brave men of the Arabian peninsula, possessing a huge number of camels which they would bring to sell in Aleppo. In summer, they lived in Busra and al-Azraq. The third 'Anza group was called al-Jallas. In summer, at the date harvest, they would head for the area surrounding Korat al-Qasīm to stock up with dates and grain.

When drought hit the land of Najd, these sub-groups of the 'Anza would head for their brethren in the land of al-Shām, who would immediately come to their aid. More than any other Arab tribe, the 'Anza were renowned for this particular trait. When Najd regained its fertility, the tribespeople would return with their families. No other place could compete with Najd at this time of year: it offered plenty of grazing land and water and a mild climate. It is worth noting that 'the entire 'Anza tribe accepted the authority of the Al Saud and perceived the rightfulness of that family's call of their own volition and mostly without wars'.[64]

Iraq viewed with the utmost concern the rivalry between Imam Abdul-

Aziz and Ibn Rashīd. King Feisal alerted Sir Percy Cox (who was now British High Commissioner in Iraq) to the fact that this rivalry was a source of concern, that it could in the long term lead to great problems regarding the demarcation of the borders of Iraq and that the victory scored by Imam Abdul-Aziz and his annexation of Hā'il exposed Iraq's southern borders to serious danger. King Feisal also informed the High Commissioner that some Najdi tribes had attacked the Zuwai' tribe, which belonged to al-Muntafik though it was settled near Zubair. The King urged Britain to take action to stop these acts of aggression, and mediate to determine the borders. Cox informed the King that he had written to the British High Commissioner in Bahrain asking him to inform Ibn Saud of these developments. But when Imam Abdul-Aziz annexed Hā'il, King Feisal grew even more concerned and demanded that the High Commissioner demarcate Iraq's southern borders without delay. Large numbers of the Shammar tribe had sought refuge in Iraq. The 'Amarat tribe, the part of 'Anza headed by Fahd bin Hathal, also sought refuge there. This angered Imam Ibn Saud, who wrote to Ibn Hathal, protesting that his authority extended to all the branches of the 'Anza tribe. This volatile situation convinced Cox that a solution to these problems must be found.[65]

The situation became even more serious when Iraq stopped its aid to the Dhufair tribe, who were scattered in an area surrounding Najd, near al-Batn. Furthermore, King Feisal appointed Yusuf al-Sa'dun to head a *hajjana* (camel corps) established in 1922 to guard Iraq's southern borders. Without hesitation, the Dhufair began to pay *zakat* to Imam Abdul-Aziz. Great numbers of the Mutair gathered in al-Hafr led by the Dawish family, a gathering which frightened the tribes, particularly the Muntafik, who expected a raid at any time. To deal with this situation, the *mutassarif* ordered those Muntafik who were with the *hajjana* to go to Abu Ghar, and started to instigate an insurgence among the tribes and get them to pay no *zakat* to Imam Abdul-Aziz. This hastened an attack by the Dawish family on Abu Ghar and the Muntafik tribes. Al-Dawish then announced that the borders of Najd were the railway lines in that area. British planes intervened, striking against the attacking Najdi tribes.[66]

These events convinced Britain that the demarcation of the borders had now become inevitable. This led to the conclusion of the Muhammara treaty, which was first rejected by Imam Abdul-Aziz, but was then ratified by him in the two protocols of al-'Uqair in 1922.

Among the most noteworthy achievements of Imam Abdul-Aziz were his intimate, expert appreciation of the tribal problem and the solutions which he put forward in harmony both with the requirements of the Saudi state and with those of the modern age. Such solutions yielded far-reaching results in

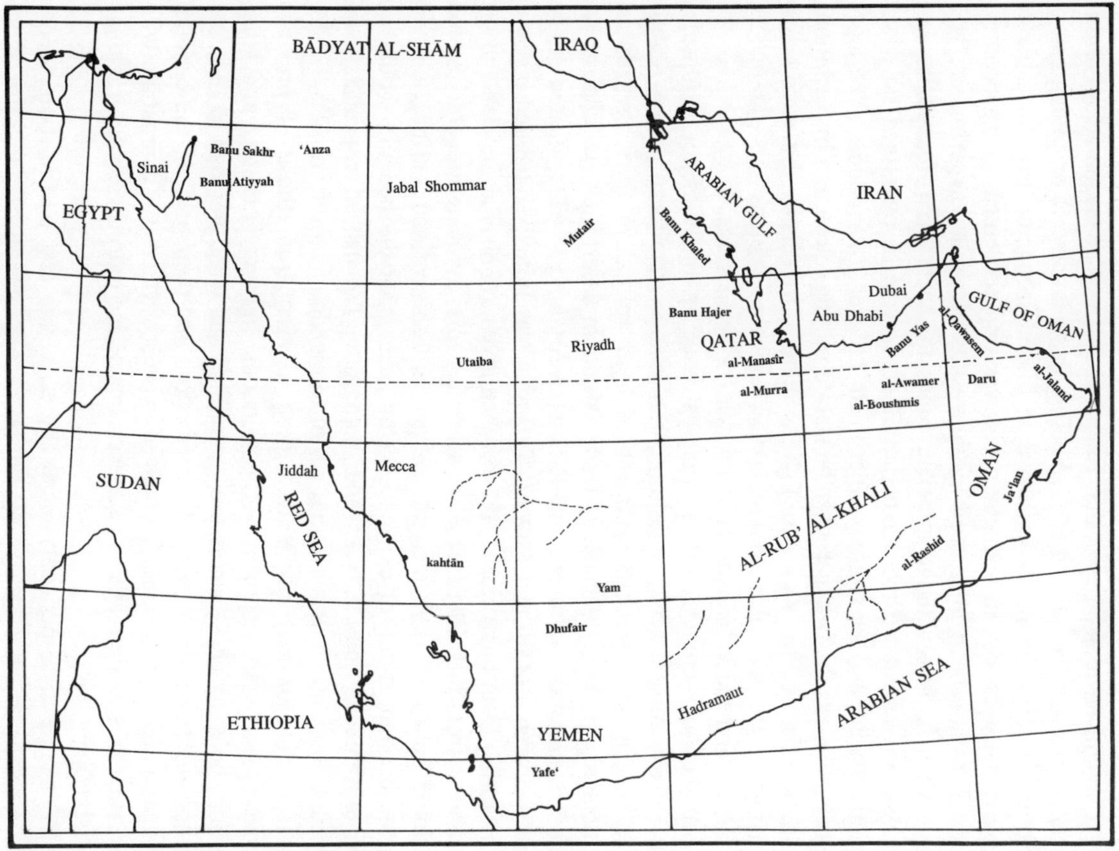

Map II. Distribution of Tribes

the political, military, economic and social fields, each of which is worthy of an independent study. It became abundantly clear that, under the state, the tribe becomes insignificant; loyalty is to the state, and the role of the tribe has long since waned and gone.[67]

It should be remembered that Imam Abdul-Aziz managed to solve this problem without having had any schooling in social studies or having had to change the basic mode of existence in his environment. He was able to achieve what he did in a manner that was unprecedented in his country, without having been influenced by the results of similar experiments; at a time when he was without sufficient funds for such a transformation; and without any assistance from experts, although what he embarked on was a unique social and economic experiment of great magnitude. Yet more remarkable was the fact that when he started putting into action his ambitious cultural scheme, he was still fighting battles to regain the state's lost territories. He was able to find a new spirit to replace the old one of tribalism and individualism passed down for generations.[68]

As bedouin culture was a complex issue in the Arabian peninsula, particularly for the newly emerging Arab Islamic state there, Imam Abdul-Aziz began with the establishment of *hijar* (plural of *hijr*, agricultural settlement), initiating the change from bedouin or desert life to sedentariness. The first *hijr* was established in 1912 on the Artawiyya wells, situated on the road between al-Zalfi and Kuwait. This area was initially inhabited by Sa'd bin Muthib from Banu Harb, and was then given to Feisal al-Dawish and his followers from the Mutair tribe. In achieving this, the King was able to bind bedouin life to the land, a significant accomplishment and a critical change in the bedouin mode of existence. This meant that the bedouin would no longer think of raids, attacks and aggression, but instead concentrate on farming the land. It was a social act of tremendous significance.[69]

It is obvious that efforts like these differed from those of previous generations. After centuries of continuous fighting, raiding, attacking, fleeing, boasting about whom they had killed and what they had looted, and composing poems eulogizing their ancestors and their origins, the bedouin settled in their *hijar*, leading a civilized existence which was compatible with the needs of a modern age and a modern state, and indeed with the teachings of Islam.

Alongside these political, social and economic results, the country now had a semi-permanent army. We thus read in the historical literature about campaigns carried out by what are referred to as brigades from the *hijar*, in addition to brigades from the towns and cities. Returning to the topic which this chapter has been addressing, we see that developments such as these constituted a final solution to the border problems.

2
Al-Ashrāf *and the First World War*

Contacts between Sherif Hussein and McMahon, the British High Commissioner in Egypt

The last decades of the nineteenth century and the early decades of the twentieth century were an important period in the history of the Ottoman Empire and its jurisdiction over the Arabs. The results of the historical developments which took place prior to this period began to emerge in the form of the 1876 constitution.

Much has been written about this period—about the autocracy of the Ottoman Sultans, and in particular that of Abdul Hamīd II. This was a period in which the Ottoman Empire was subjected to an intellectual onslaught from Europe in general and from France in particular. Non-Muslims played a critical role in this endeavour; the repercussions of this were felt most clearly in al-Shām, and particularly in Lebanon. This was partly because of Lebanon's unique demographic, intellectual and ideological situation and partly because of the special system worked out just after the mid-nineteenth century by an international commission. The new system stipulated that the country would be run by a Christian *mutassarif* to be appointed by the Sultan and approved by the European states, and that a council would be formed which included members representing the Druse, the Maronites, the Greek Orthodox and the Roman Catholics. The European states thus used the issue of non-Muslim confessional groups as a pretext for intervention in the internal affairs of Lebanon.

This period also saw the rise of Midhat Pasha, who filled a number of senior positions in the Ottoman administration, moving between Lebanon, Paris, Vienna and Brussels. He was appointed Grand Vizier under the Ottoman Sultan Abdul-Aziz (who ruled from 1861), but then sought with a number of colleagues to obtain a *fatwa* (religious ruling) allowing the deposition of the Sultan. Sultan Abdul-Aziz was replaced by his younger brother, Abdul Hamīd II, who began his reign by appointing Midhat Grand Vizier and proclaiming the constitution. The constitution stipulated that a parliamentary government be established, and that the parliament consist of two councils: the Council of Deputies and the Council of Senators. But faced with a deteriorating situation and the fact that the Empire was forced to accept a humiliating reconciliation with Russia in the treaty of San Stefano in 1878, together with the Armenian dissension, the Sultan suspended the constitution and dissolved parliament, calling instead for an Islamic League. This movement is referred to by some historians as the Hamīdi coup.[1]

Historical developments rolled on, giving rise in this period to the notion of Turkish nationalism and the Turkish Youth Movement (Turkiyya al-Fatat). This movement began to operate from within the Empire itself in the reign of Abdul Hamīd II. But when its clandestine activities were uncovered, its leaders were exiled, choosing to live in Paris, Cairo and Geneva, where they had their own newspapers, *Mashurat*, *Mizan* and *Othmanli*. By then, the movement had adopted a new name, the Ottoman Society of Union and Progress (al-Ittihad wa al-Taraqqi). Its programme was precisely the one proclaimed in *Mashurat*: reforms on the model of the European system, and the Ottomanization or Turkification of other nationalities.

After their leaders were exiled, the nationalists began to form underground cells, particularly among the Turkish army. The most important of these cells was the Nation and Freedom Society (al-Watan wa al-Hurriyya), first established in Damascus by Mustafa Kemal (Ataturk) from among the officers of the Fifth Ottoman Army stationed in al-Shām at the time. These continued to demand that the constitution be restored until this was granted in 1908. In the new Council, the Society of Union and Progress was surprised by the formation of a counter-bloc under the name of the Party of Free People (Hizb al-Ahrar), which called for decentralization, an antithesis to the centralism for which the Society of Union and Progress had been calling. In a reaction to this development, a new party came into being: the Islamic Union Party (al-Ittihad al-Islami), which regarded the constitution as an act which contravened the Shari‘a.

In these circumstances, some members of the Union and Progress Society and of the Party of Free People were assassinated. In 1909 pro-Union and

Progress troops occupied the capital, intent on killing the Sultan. But the people greeted them with the slogan, 'Long live the Sultan.' Consequently, the Council of Deputies and the Council of Senators were combined to form a National Society, which was then forced to remove Sultan Abdul Hamīd and grant his brother Rashad the title Sultan Muhammad V. The situation remained unchanged under the Unionists until the First World War.

The Turanian nationalistic orientation meant that a policy of Turkification was adopted, leading to the supersession of the Arabic alphabet, language and culture. In the Council of Deputies, the Arabic language was constantly under attack. When one of the Arab members proposed that the use of Arabic be made obligatory for government officials appointed in Arab states, the proposal was flatly rejected.

Faced with such policies of Turkification, Arab leaders were suspicious of the sincerity of the Union and Progress Society, which was expected to issue a genuine call for freedom, reform and equality. In fact, these Arab doubts and fears in relation to the Unionists became an integral part of Arab policy once Turanian extremism and Turkish nationalism had revealed their true colours and persisted in challenging Arab dignity.

The suspicions of the Arabs and the difficulty of their position were exacerbated by the removal of Sultan Abdul Hamīd II, which also led to the removal of senior Arab officials on whom the Arabs could rely. These were accused of being behind what was referred to as the Sultan's regime. The situation was thus different from that in the days of the old Sultan, who had sought to win over the Arab elements by appointing them to the most senior and sensitive positions. The Sultan had brought these elements so close to him that they had a decisive influence in government.

The removal of Sultan Abdul Hamīd, however, underlined the basic fact that the Unionists were unable to prevent the loss of certain parts of the Empire; no sooner had they taken over than the balance was lost and disintegration set in without their being aware of it. Some of the Unionists acknowledged this failure and their lack of knowledge of the way that affairs of state were handled.[2] It was indeed as though the Ottoman Empire were being gradually severed from the Arab world, although, as a great Islamic state, the Empire was established and consolidated on the basis that Arab areas would form the most prominent part. Arabic is the language of the Qur'ān and Islam's two holy shrines happen to be in one of the Arab lands.

The Arab nationalist movement had been gaining momentum in al-Shām ever since the beginning of the nineteenth century. Nasīf al-Yāziji and Butrus al-Bustani contributed to this process. The political press and scholarly journals played an important role in spreading the idea of Arab nationalism. Al-Yāziji published two journals, *al-Bayan* and *al-Diya'*;

Ahmad Faris al-Shidyaq, originally a Christian, published a weekly newspaper, *al-Jawa'ib*; the Jesuit fathers in Beirut published a weekly newspaper, *al-Bashīr*; and the Maronites, the Protestants and the Orthodox published newspapers of their own. The appearance of these newspapers led to the widespread use of the printing press, which played a significant role. Foreign missionaries also became active in this period.

In al-Shām, too, a group of Arab secular intellectuals emerged, including Farah Anton from Tripoli (in present-day Lebanon) and Muhammad Rashīd, a Syrian, who, although akin to Jamal al-Din al-Afghani and Muhammad Abduh in calling for the renaissance of the Arab nation and the principles of early Islam to be put into practice, differed from these thinkers in also calling for Arab nationalism. In a number of issues of his *al-Manar*, he took the side of the Arab Ottomans, demanding, like them, self-government within an Ottoman framework. He contributed to the establishment of the Ottoman Decentralist Party, founded in Cairo in 1912 with the aim of urging the Turkish rulers to adopt a decentralized system of government. Arab nationalist feeling was even more apparent in the writings of Abdul-Rahman al-Kawakibi, particularly in his two books, *Umm al-Qura* and *Taba'i' al-Istibdad*.

The results of all this were to be embodied in the resolutions of the first Arab Conference which opened on 18 June 1913 in the Assembly Hall of the Geographical Society in Paris. These called for active Arab participation in the decentralized administration and stipulated that a decentralized administration be set up in every Arab state, that Arabic be recognized as a working language in the Ottoman parliament, and that Arabic be the official language and the language of education in the Arab states.[3]

The extremist Turanian movement was characterized by the notion of the supremacy of the Turkish people and the desire to rid Turkish culture of Arab and Persian influence. In the period which preceded the First World War, the Unionists stringently applied these principles which, in effect, reversed all the principles on which the Empire had been founded.

The Arabs saw that the new situation of Turkification and centralization posed a threat to them, particularly to their Arab and Islamic culture. Some Arabs saw this as a threat to what they called Arab nationalism and consequently called for a decentralized system of government which would leave the various Arab areas within the entity of the Empire and at the same time preserve the Arab identity, particularly Arabic language and culture. The Arab societies grew more active, including al-Fatat, al-'Ahd and al-Jami'a al-Qahtaniyya.[4]

In the period preceding the First World War, Italy was seeking a colonizing role. Its troops landed in Ottoman North Africa with the intention of occupying Tripoli. Although the Arab inhabitants sided enthusiastically with the Ottomans, they were finally defeated and were forced to relinquish Tripoli and Benghazi, which came under Italian control in 1912.

In the same year, rebellion erupted against Ottoman rule in the Balkans when the Balkan states revolted. This was a rebuttal of the proposals of the centralist Unionists, who were seeking to link Macedonia indissolubly with the Empire. The Ottomans were forced to accept a humiliating reconciliation. This, in turn, led the Unionists to become more extremist and adopt drastic notions such as Turanian nationalism as an all-encompassing ideal and Turkification or total adherence to the idea of nationalism in response to the intellectual onslaught from outside referred to above.[5]

Counteracting the Unionists' insistence on the idea of Turkification and Turanian nationalism, reacting to their defeat by Italy in Tripoli, and echoing the secessionist nationalist movement in the Balkans, the leaders of the Arab organizations al-Fatat[6] and al-'Ahd called for an independent Arab state, whose borders would extend from the Mersin–Adana line to the Iranian border in the north; from the Iranian border to the Arabian Gulf in the east, and to the Indian Ocean in the south; and along the Red Sea and then the Mediterranean to Mersin in the west.

In 1876, at the beginning of the reign of Sultan Abdul Hamīd II, a law was issued known as the 'Law of the States' or the 'Basic Ottoman Law of the Lands of the Ottoman Empire'. This law provided for the division of the Empire into areas called *vilayets*, and these into provinces (*mutassarifiyyas*), which were then divided into administrative districts (*qā'imaqamiyyas*) and these in turn into a number of smaller areas (*nawāhis*). The law also provided for the election of committees to assist the governor (*wāli*), the provincial governor (*mutassarif*) and the administrative officer (*qā'imaqām*). It regulated the system of justice by creating regular courts and religious courts, ruled on tax collection and expenditure, and finally created Fund Councils whose task in every district was to look into *waqf* (religious endowment), its administration and its expenditure. Typically, the Unionists tended to apply this law as rigorously as possible in their desire to consolidate the Empire's grip on the other lands, an effort which in effect meant neutralizing the authority of the Sherif of Mecca in that province.

It was then that Sherif Hussein started to entertain the idea of working to achieve independence from the Ottoman Empire, which was also the Caliphate. With this aim in mind, he began contacting the British. A meeting between Sherif Hussein's son Emir Abdullah and Lord Kitchener, the British High Commissioner in Cairo, set the process in motion in 1912.[7]

The foregoing may perhaps shed light on the significance of the emergence of the Salafi Arab state, represented by the Sultanate of Najd and led by Imam Abdul-Aziz, and on the fact that this man and his state managed to steer clear of the prevalent intellectual and political upheaval in the Ottoman Empire, of the European intellectual onslaught and of the ills that befell a large number of the Arab lands. Abdul-Aziz's adherence to a position of neutrality in these struggles, both before and during the First World War, was of immense benefit to the Arabs.

Britain tried to use the nationalist movement in some parts of the Arab East to its own advantage. With the Indian experience fresh in its mind, Britain was aware of the importance of the Islamic movement. It was also watching carefully and fearfully the increasing influence of Germany in the Ottoman Empire, as demonstrated by the Berlin–Baghdad railway line. This venture particularly threatened Britain's standing in the Arabian Gulf and India. Moreover, if Turkey were suddenly to be at war with Britain, this would pose a threat to the British Empire's communication links through Aden and Suez. Finally, Britain feared that the Ottoman Sultan (who was also the Muslim Caliph) would declare a *jihad* (holy war). Given this situation, the British decided to incite the Arabs against the Ottoman Empire and planned to meet with Arab nationalists who were keen on separation from it.[8]

Primarily because of the position of Hejaz, the Sherif of Mecca, Hussein bin Ali, was Britain's choice to lead the revolt against the Turks. The decision was made by the Arab Bureau in Cairo.[9] The British Government of India was worried about inciting the Arabs against the Ottoman Caliphate for fear of undesirable repercussions among the Muslims of India. Sherif Hussein, on the other hand, had already been seeking, as mentioned above, to establish an Arab Kingdom with Britain's help. Thus, there were negotiations between Sherif Hussein and Sir Henry McMahon, the British High Commissioner in Egypt and Sudan from 1914 to 1916. At these meetings, Hussein went beyond his mandate as an Emir and a Sherif in Hejaz, behaving as though he were the King of the Arabs, the representative of the nationalist movement referred to above and the prospective Caliph of the Muslim world.

Britain was confident about its policy design and the feasibility of implementing it and its representative in Egypt was given a free hand. McMahon, who had succeeded Lord Kitchener in Cairo, proceeded to offer Sherif Hussein the Caliphate, if he would only declare a revolt against the Turks. To pursue this aim, McMahon used three of his officers: Storrs, Hogarth and Lawrence.[10]

In September 1914 Lord Kitchener, the Secretary of State for War, instructed the mission in Cairo to make contact with Sherif Hussein. McMahon attended to the matter, assisted by three experts in Arab affairs:

Reginald Wingate, the Governor-General of Sudan; Ronald Storrs, the Oriental Secretary; and Gilbert Clayton, head of intelligence in Cairo.[11]

When the First World War broke out in 1914, Imam Abdul-Aziz feared that the raging struggle would reach the Arabian peninsula, where people were loyal to various rulers, and it could lead to the entire peninsula going up in flames not of its own making. He thus wrote to his three neighbours, Ibn Rashīd, Sherif Hussein and Sheikh Mubarak, inviting them to a meeting at which they could consult with one another and reach an agreement that could spare the Arabs this calamitous war. Although the attempt was unsuccessful, the Imam's adherence to neutrality never faltered. He left Sherif Hussein to his own devices in Hejaz, and did not step in the way of the Ottoman troops in 'Asīr and Yemen, permitting their messengers freedom of movement between Yemen and al-Shām.[12]

With pressure mounting on the battle-front, the Allies sought to incite the Arabs against the Turks. The British government instructed its representatives and others to make contact with the Arab leaders in the various capitals; hence the treaty with al-Idrisi in 'Asīr in 1915.

A reconciliation had been achieved between the Ottoman authorities and Imam Yahya of Yemen in 1911, involving Yahya's acceptance of Ottoman sovereignty in return for an annual hand-out. In response, al-Idrisi, who was on bad terms with Imam Yahya, decided to cut the Rumma supply lines and lay siege to the capital of 'Asīr and the Ottomans' command centre, the town of Abha. He did so because the Turks had not sought a similar reconciliation with him. Al-Idrisi then turned to the British, welcoming negotiations with the rulers of Aden and wasting no time in making an alliance in a treaty concluded on 30 April 1915.[13]

In response, Britain embarked on negotiations with Sherif Hussein in Hejaz. At the same time, McMahon established the Arab Bureau in Cairo and entrusted Clayton with the task of directing it, in order to study the development of British policy in Arab affairs and follow up its inplementation.[14]

During this period, British policy in the Arab world was designed by two agencies: the British Government of India and the Arab Bureau. The former concerned itself with Arab affairs relating to the east of the peninsula, the Arabian Gulf and Iraq. The Arab Bureau, on the other hand, was concerned with affairs relating to the rest of the Arab world. The viewpoints of the two sides were often in conflict regarding issues that did not come exclusively within the remit of either.

Lord Kitchener[15] wrote to Sherif Hussein, sounding him out on where he would stand if Turkey decided to enter the war against the Allies. The question was coupled with a British promise to help the Arabs achieve independence. Added to this was the guarantee that 'Britain will defend the right of Sherif Hussein to the throne, will protect him from any aggression, and will recognize him as the Caliph of the Muslims if and when he is elected.' Sherif Hussein's reply to Lord Kitchener expressed his desire to enter into an alliance with Britain. The reply was sent secretly through the Arab Bureau in Cairo.[16]

Thus, Ibn Rashīd and Imam Yahya sided with the Turks, while Sherif Hussein, al-Idrisi and Sheikh Mubarak, the Emir of Kuwait, sided with Britain. Imam Abdul-Aziz, however, sided with neither party, staunchly adhering to his policy of neutrality.

This also signalled the start of what came to be known as the Hussein-McMahon correspondence. The process was set in motion with a memorandum which Sherif Hussein sent to McMahon in the middle of 1915, speaking on behalf of the Arab nation, and offering Britain the assistance of the Arabs if it was prepared to assist them in achieving the independence of the entire Arab peninsula and declare its endorsement of the establishment of an Arab Caliphate. McMahon's reply stated that Britain would not object to the transfer of the Caliphate to Sherif Hussein. Britain's policy then hinged on the necessity of keeping the Islamic holy places in the hands of an independent state and avoiding offence to Muslims, particularly those of India.[17]

As for the borders of the Arab state to which Sherif Hussein referred in his memorandum, McMahon—relying on a drawing which determined the borders of the new state and which the leaders of al-Fatat and al-'Ahd had given him—maintained that it was premature to determine the final borders of an independent Arab state. The reason for this, he argued, was that some Arabs were still fighting on the side of the Turks. He was perhaps referring to Ibn Rashīd and Imam Yahya. But whatever the reasons, McMahon insisted that the time had not yet come for a demarcation of the borders of the new state which was to be granted independence.[18]

Although the Hussein–McMahon correspondence continued until the end of January 1916, Hussein did not obtain a firm promise as McMahon postponed making such a commitment, taking into consideration the interests of the French.[19] In January 1916, however, the two parties eventually signed an agreement which consisted of the following five articles:

1. Britain undertakes to form an Arab government which is independent in the full sense of the word, both internally and externally. The borders of this state shall be the Persian Gulf in the east; the Red Sea, the Egyptian border and the Mediterranean in the west; and the northern borders of Aleppo and Mosul until the confluence of the Euphrates and

the Tigris at the mouth of the Persian Gulf. Only the colony of Aden shall be excluded from this demarcation.

2. Britain undertakes to protect and maintain this government against any interference, whatever form this may take, whether internal or external, by protecting its land and sea borders against all acts of aggression.

3. The Basra *vilayet* shall be under the supervision of Britain until the new government completes its reorganization. In return for this supervision, and bearing in mind the position of the new government, Britain shall be paid a sum of money.

4. Britain undertakes to supply the new Arab government with all its requirements of arms, ammunition and funds throughout the war period.

5. Britain undertakes to cut off the supply line from Mersin or from a suitable cut-off point in that area to lighten the war burden on those not prepared for it.[20]

In addition to these undertakings, Britain promised to recognize Hussein as the Muslim Caliph when he was elected as such. In June 1916 the Sherif of Mecca declared the revolt against the Turks.[21]

The Hussein–McMahon correspondence was published in London in 1939 under the title *Correspondence between Sir Henry McMahon, His Majesty's High Commissioner at Cairo, and the Sherif Hussein of Mecca, July 1915* (md. 5951, mis. no. 3, 1939).

At the same time, contacts were under way between Britain and France regarding the fate of the Ottoman dependencies. Britain was represented by Sir Mark Sykes, a British expert on Middle Eastern affairs, while France was represented by François Georges-Picot, the French Consul-General in Beirut before the First World War. This was part of the extensive contacts which took place between Russia, Britain and France to apportion the territories of the Ottoman Empire.[22]

The British and French representatives completed the preparation of their proposal towards the end of February 1916 and took this to Petrograd to discuss with the Russian government. Meanwhile, Russia had requested that it be the protector of Orthodox Christian interests in Palestine. The interests of the three states clashed regarding Palestine. These differences were eventually resolved with the decision to establish an international administration in Jerusalem, and put Palestine under British control. In return for this, France would receive the lands which are now known as Syria and Lebanon. Finally, the Russians would be compensated with areas of influence in north-east Anatolia.[23]

This agreement was ratified in April 1916 by the three states. Sazanov, the Russian Foreign Minister, took part. As mentioned above, the agreement provided for the establishment of direct rule by the French over the Syrian coast, and by the British over the two *vilayets* of Basra and Baghdad. The northern part of the Syrian interior and the *vilayet* of Basra were to await the recognition of an independent Arab state, in which France would enjoy the right to offer economic and consultative assistance. Another independent Arab state would be established in the inner part of the area under British control.[24] The agreement also expressed the readiness of France and Britain to protect an independent Arab state or an alliance of Arab states headed by an Arab President in the two interior areas of Iraq and Syria.[25]

The Arab Bureau directed T.E. Lawrence[26] to head for Hejaz, and Lawrence, in turn, directed Emir Feisal bin Hussein to mobilize his troops north of Yanbu‘. The aim of this mobilization was twofold: to make possible an attack on the Hejaz railway line, and consequently a frontal assault on the Turkish troops as they retreated; and to enable Allenby's troops to advance to the Sinai peninsula and Palestine. With these plans in mind, Lawrence and Feisal advanced on Damascus in November 1918.[27]

While Feisal and Abdullah were in the thick of battle with the Turks, their father, Sherif Hussein, was preoccupied both with consolidating his throne in Hejaz and with winning over the dignitaries of Mecca and persuading them to proclaim him King of the Arabs on 29 October 1916. This was to ensure that the 1916 agreement (which had so far only been signed) did in fact come into effect as the outcome of his own correspondence with McMahon. From that date, in all correspondence, Hussein began to call himself Sherif and Emir of Mecca, and King of the Arabs. But Hussein was soon to be bitterly disappointed. Britain, France and Italy would recognize him only as King of Hejaz. This was stated in a joint memorandum which the three countries sent him on 3 January 1917.[28]

A bigger shock came with the Balfour Declaration[29] of 2 November 1917. This provided for the establishment of a 'national home' for the Jews in Palestine. The declaration was followed by a message from the British Foreign Office to Hussein, through Hogarth in the Arab Bureau, informing him that the existence of the Jews in Palestine was not in conflict with the interests of the Arab population of Palestine. To lessen the blow of the Balfour Declaration, Britain and France also issued a joint communiqué stating that their aim, which was to liberate the peoples of the region from Ottoman rule, had now been realized and that from that date they were ready to establish independent governments in both Syria and Iraq.[30]

The Petrograd contacts and the Sykes–Picot agreement remained secret until the October 1917 revolution. Russia withdrew from the war, and the texts of the secret agreements and treaties previously concluded were made public.[31] These revelations shocked the Arabs in general, and Hussein in particular.[32] But Hussein was once again to be taken aback when Wilson, the US President, announced in a speech in 1918 that one of the principles which the US had adhered to when entering the war was not to recognize secret agreements between the Allies.

The First World War ended, an armistice was announced and the Turks finally surrendered in October 1918, followed by Germany in November. The Paris Peace Conference opened in January 1919. Instead of attending to the successive blows he had been dealt and the unfulfilled promises he had been given, Hussein concentrated all his attention on the peace conference. He sent his son Feisal to attend on his behalf, still hoping that the conference would accede to his demands.[33]

To counteract Allied conspiracies against the Arab cause which were beginning to come to light, the Damascus Conference was held in the first week of March 1920. The conference announced the independence of Syria, including Lebanon, Palestine and what was later known as Transjordan.

It was on this occasion that Britain fully appreciated how important it was to reach a speedy understanding with France. The two countries thus hastened to convene, in San Remo[34] in April 1920, what they called the Supreme Council of the Allies. At this conference, and in a settlement reached on 25 April 1920, Britain agreed to a French mandate over Syria and Lebanon. Iraq was to be under a British mandate, and so was Palestine, in accordance with Article 22 of the League of Nations Charter.[35]

This was the settlement which France insisted on completing before concluding the agreement on oil and oilfields in the *vilayet* of Mosul. In accordance with this agreement, France conceded Mosul and its oilfields to Britain, in return for a French mandate over Syria and Lebanon.

The Mandate and the Extension of al-Ashrāf *Rule to Iraq and Transjordan*

As for the mandate, it could be said that the First World War was merely a struggle between two groups of colonial powers, competing to control the destiny of the world. The mandate system may thus be viewed as a form of colonization which masked the underlying greed. The historical developments which took place before and during the war led the colonial powers to think up and pursue new methods which could ensure their survival.

The real aim behind the mandate system was to assist those countries victorious in the First World War to achieve their war aims, which were the annexation of German colonies and the sharing out of Ottoman lands. It was thus a new form of colonization.

General Smuts, once Prime Minister of South Africa, wrote a book on the subject entitled *The League of Nations: Practical Proposals*, in which he expounded his ideas on Article 119 of the Treaty of Versailles, and suggested that land belonging to defeated countries must be annexed and brought under the authority of the League of Nations and that the League, in turn, could transfer that authority to any country it chose. In his book, Smuts was trying to reconcile international legitimacy and the desire to control colonies. He was representing South Africa and was thus seeking to justify the handing over of German South-West Africa[36] to South Africa as a reward for fighting alongside the Allies. The mandate system can thus be seen as nothing more than masked colonization, with the League of Nations entrusting some of the victorious countries with the administration of lands and colonies.[37]

Mandates took three basic forms: (a) mandates over relatively developed nations such as those under the Ottoman Empire which were then governed by their own people with guidance from the mandating countries; (b) mandates over less developed nations, such as those of East Africa, in which the mandating countries were allowed to administer the affairs of their colonies; and (c) mandates over undeveloped nations, in which the mandating countries were allowed to exercise direct rule and establish a comprehensive administration.

Thus, the preamble to Article 22 of the League of Nations Charter contained the following provision:

> Lands which as a result of the last war are no longer under the control of their governments before the war, and which are inhabited by people who cannot keep pace with the requirements of the modern age, are best and most practically placed under the mandate of civilized peoples whose resources, experience and geographical position would enable them willingly to carry the burden, provided that mandating a particular country to supervise those peoples referred to in this article is solely the responsibility of the League of Nations.

Thus, mandates ostensibly meant assisting peoples. In reality, however, they meant the acquisition of new colonies, which was a procedure similar to that adopted in the wake of the Second World War, the only difference being one of terminology, changing the mandate system to one of trusteeship.[38] The mandate system became part and parcel of the League of Nations Charter. Article 22 of the Charter came to embody its meaning and aims, and the methods by which it was implemented.

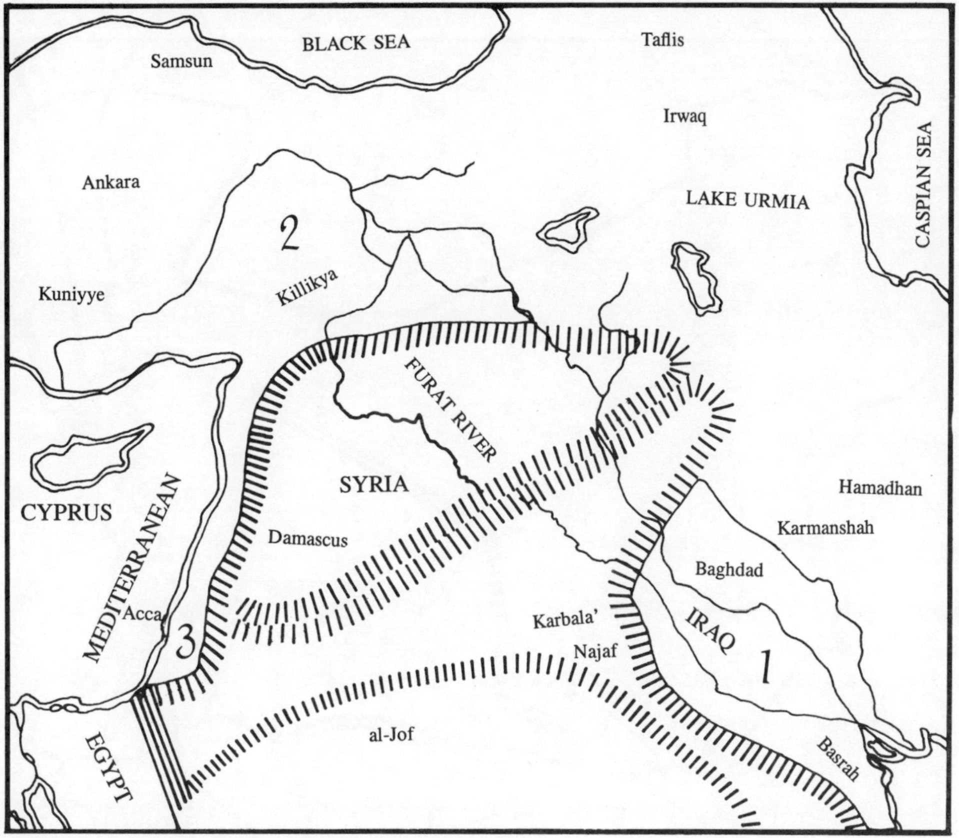

Map III. The Sykes–Picot Agreement, 1916

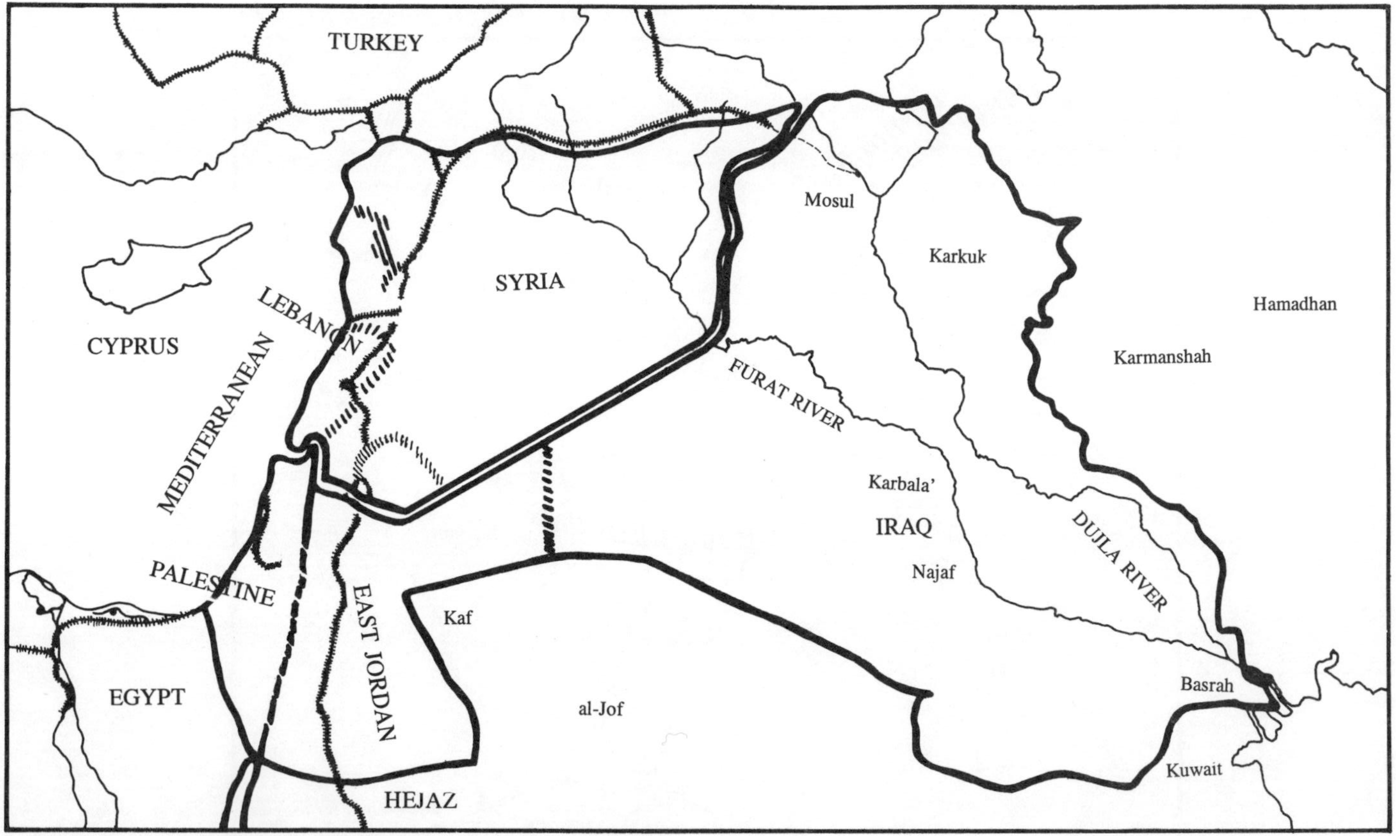

Map IV. Decisions of the San Remo Conference, 1920

Article 22 of the League of Nations Charter provided that the colonies and countries which as a result of the war were no longer dependent on the states which had formerly ruled them, and which were inhabited by peoples who were unable by themselves to cope with the urgent requirements of the modern world, should have applied to them the principle according to which the prosperity and progress of such peoples were the inviolable responsibility of the entire civilized world, which must guarantee the fulfilment of such a responsibility. This undertaking included the following three corollaries:

> 1. The best means of putting into practice this principle is that such peoples be placed under the trusteeship of nations of the civilized world which, by virtue of their resources, experience and geographical position, are ideally placed to accept and shoulder this responsibility. These developed nations must exercise their trusteeship responsibilities as mandating states acting on behalf of the League of Nations.
>
> 2. The form which mandates take must vary with the degree of development, the geographical position and the economic conditions of the underdeveloped peoples in question.
>
> 3. Those peoples who were under the Turkish Empire[39] have achieved a degree of progress which qualifies them to be temporarily recognized as independent entities, but shall continue to receive administrative guidance and other forms of assistance from the mandating states until such time as they are able to fend for themselves. The wishes of these peoples shall be taken into prime consideration in the choice of the mandating state.[40]

Thus, mandate type *c* (see p. 42) is the closest of the three types of mandate to traditional flagrant colonization.

Article 22 also stipulated that:

> Every time a mandate is imposed, the mandating state shall submit to the council an annual report on the country put under it. The degree of authority, supervision and administration exercised by the mandating state, if not already agreed to by the League of Nations, must be explicitly determined and for each case by the council.

Thus, it was found necessary to establish a permanent committee to receive and examine the annual reports submitted by the mandating states, and to advise on all matters relating to the mandate.[41]

This is how the destiny of the Arab states was being shaped: first by the Petrograd agreement, then by the Sykes–Picot agreement and finally by the resolutions of the San Remo Conference. Here, the Supreme Council of the Allies met at the Rofashan Palace, which was owned by a Briton who had spent much of his life in British India. *Rofashan* means 'the sky of paradise' or, as the owner would have it, 'the haven of happiness', as though the happiness of Britain and France lay in the devouring of the Arab states under the term 'mandate'.[42]

The peace treaty, the treaty of Sèvres, was imposed on the Turks by the Allies and signed in August 1920. But after their subsequent victories in Anatolia, the Turks forced the Allies to accept the treaty of Lucerne, concluded in January 1923.

When his hopes were thwarted at the peace conference, Sherif Hussein refused to recognize the treaties of Versailles and Sèvres. This refusal led to his non-participation in the Lucerne Conference.[43]

At the peace conference, the Arab delegates considered the resolutions of San Remo a betrayal of their cause. The Hejazi delegation submitted a formal protest, first to the conference, and then to the League of Nations.

This was followed by a conference in which British politicians and military strategists deliberated and laid down the ground rules for dealing with the Arab issue. The conference was held in March 1921 in Cairo, in the light of directives from the Arab Bureau, and with the resolutions of the San Remo Conference in mind.

In August of the same year, Lawrence was dispatched to Jiddah to conclude a treaty with Sherif Hussein which would make him recognize the mandate imposed on both Syria and Iraq, in return for the financial aid that had already been given. Smarting under Britain's perfidy, Hussein refused to give Lawrence a positive response.[44]

Reference has already been made to the British army moving into Damascus together with the Arab army led by Feisal bin Hussein. The people of al-Shām thought that, given the promises made by Britain to Sherif Hussein before his revolt, the time had come to establish an independent Arab state. The Arab forces entered Damascus on 30 September 1918 and proclaimed an Arab state. They were unaware, however, that secret agreements had been concluded at San Remo to partition Syria, giving France the right to occupy Syria and Lebanon and impose its mandate on them.[45]

At the end of the Ottoman era, Syria was administratively divided into three *vilayets* (Aleppo, Damascus and Beirut), two *mutassarifiyyas* directly attached to the Ministry of Interior (Jerusalem and Deir ez-Zor) and, in accordance with a special statute agreed between the Ottoman Empire and the European states, a supreme *mutassarifiyya* attached to the office of the Grand Vizier (the *mutassarifiyya* of the independent Mount Lebanon).[46]

Hussein's sons endeavoured to salvage what they could. Feisal bin Hussein, for his part, aimed to be the head of a state within the Syrian interior. In November 1918 he left for London to negotiate with the British Foreign Secretary, Lord Curzon. In February of the following year, Feisal defended the Arabs' right to independence at the Paris Peace Conference. In response to a proposal from President Wilson, it was decided that a commission of inquiry composed of two US experts (the King–Crane Commission) be dispatched to Syria. Feisal returned to Syria and began to work against France.

The Arab Youth Society (al-'Arabiyya al-Fatat) changed its name to the Arab Independence Party, and there was also a change in the concept of nationalism, from the idea of Arab unity to the idea of Syria as independent of Hejaz, and also of an independent Iraq. A conference was held, demanding Syria's independence under Feisal and rejecting the mandate outright. The report of the King–Crane Commission endorsed the notion of Syria under Feisal's rule, but recommended maintaining the mandate.[47]

On 8 March 1920 a national conference was held in Damascus, proclaiming Feisal King of Syria. As mentioned earlier, however, the San Remo Conference on 25 April 1920 had entrusted France with the mandate over the whole of Syria. Moreover, on 14 July 1920, General Gouraud, the Commander of the French troops in Lebanon, issued a warning to King Feisal that he should recognize the French mandate. General disturbances ensued, and Feisal rejected the French warning.

In the following month, the treaty of Sèvres referred to Syria as an independent state under French mandate.[48] French troops landed on the Lebanese coast and moved in the direction of Damascus, engaging the Arab troops at Maisalun and forcing Feisal to leave Damascus.

In this tense atmosphere, Britain convened a conference in Cairo in 1921, which was attended by senior politicians and military strategists and presided over by Winston Churchill, the British Foreign Secretary. The conference resolved that a monarchy be established in Iraq under a British mandate and that Feisal bin Hussein be King of Iraq. The conference also agreed to the establishment of an Emirate in Transjordan, with Abdullah bin Hussein as Emir.

Nothing is perhaps more indicative of the consolidation of Imam Abdul-Aziz's position than Britain's recognition of him as the Sultan of Najd and its Dependencies, after years of referring to him as the ruler of Najd and the chief of its tribes.[49]

Britain considered Iraq particularly important for its own interests. Britain's trade and links with its colonies in India were sustainable via two main routes. The first and most important extended from the Arabian Gulf, through Mesopotamia and on to the Mediterranean via either Syria or Anatolia. Iraq was also of crucial strategic significance, which made Basra and Mosul particularly important. Furthermore, British control of Iraq would in effect mean thwarting the Berlin–Baghdad railway project which the Germans intended to pursue in order to provide Germany with access to the Arabian Gulf.[50]

During the First World War, Iraq was occupied by an Anglo-Indian army to protect what Britain called its vital interests in the Gulf. This army took Basra first and established an administration along the lines of that in India.[51] Emir Feisal reached Basra on 23 June 1921. An *ad hoc* referendum was conducted and, on 22 August 1921, Feisal was proclaimed King of Iraq. As the British military administration had been in the hands of the British Government of India, Iraq was still outside Allenby's administrative area. Moreover, as previously pointed out, Iraq had been a 'category *a*' state (i.e. a former Turkish possession) in terms of the kinds of mandate proposed by the San Remo Conference. This enabled Sir Percy Cox, the British High Commissioner in Iraq, to implement the mandate system immediately.[52]

The first article of the Iraqi mandate document stipulated that the mandating state should, as soon as possible and within three years from the date of implementing the mandate, issue a basic statute for Iraq, to be referred to the Council of the League of Nations for ratification. This meant that by March 1923, Iraq would have its own law. The law, which was ratified by the King in March 1925, was tantamount to a constitution, particularly as there was a tendency in certain quarters to treat it as such.

The elections for the constituent assembly under this constitution took place in October 1922. However, because of the resistance of Shiah leaders, the assembly did not convene until March 1924; after heated discussions, it was able to approve the British–Iraqi treaty which had been agreed in the 1922 negotiations, leading to increasing opposition to the mandate and the treaty itself. The Iraqi constitution was published in its final form only in March 1925. The treaty, on the other hand, was ratified by Abdul Rahman al-Naqib's government, which was formed in 1922; it was to come into effect upon the exchange of the ratification instruments by the two parties, and after the constituent assembly had accepted it. This council was convened in March 1924, and Britain undertook to nominate Iraq for membership of the League of Nations.[53]

Britain subsequently concentrated its efforts on two issues. The first issue was calming the situation to bring about the internal security necessary for it to prepare for any exigencies that might arise *vis-à-vis* Turkey, and organizing the independence of Iraq as best it could to support its military effort. Britain had ended the war financially burdened, and wished to avoid further problems that might prove costly in both financial and military terms. Hence Britain's plan to resort to measures that could secure its presence in the area at the least possible cost. These measures involved putting Iraq under the Colonial Office instead of the British Government of India and appointing a High Commissioner there. The second issue over which Britain was to exert a concerted effort was the demarcation of the borders, in order to qualify Iraq for membership of the League of Nations.[54]

The countries east of the river Jordan were part of Syria. Britain added these to its own possessions in order to form a buffer zone facing the Sultanate of Najd and its Dependencies, and to secure access to Iraq. Abdullah bin Hussein arrived at the head of a small bedouin force and met with tribal chieftains in the town of Salt in July 1920. In March of the same year, he had been declared Emir of Transjordan. The British recognized his Emirate, on condition that he conclude a treaty with Britain regarding the mandate.[55]

So far, this chapter has examined the situation in the Ottoman Empire just before and during the First World War, the policy of Britain and the Allies, the development of the concept of Turkish nationalism and that of its counterpart—Arab nationalism—and finally the Hussein–McMahon correspondence, the Petrograd contacts, the Sykes–Picot agreement, the Paris Peace Conference and the San Remo agreement, together with the creation of the new political entities which resulted from these pacts to the north of the Arabian peninsula: under the British mandate in Iraq, Palestine and Transjordan, and under the French mandate in Syria and Lebanon.

These political entities were new in the sense that they had never previously had established, known or accepted borders, particularly in the south. In the past, they were all part of the Ottoman Empire, or were *vilayets* within the Empire. The establishment of these new states in the wake of the First World War created the problem of border demarcation, particularly with the newly emerging state under Imam Sultan Abdul-Aziz.

All these new states were mandated territories, two of them (Iraq and Transjordan) under a British mandate bordering the Sultanate of Najd. After the annexation of Hā'il, the subjugation of the Jabal and the advance towards al-Jof and Wādī al-Sarhan, the Sultanate of Najd and its Dependencies came to border the two states under the British mandate. This meant that the new borders were neither definite nor geographically demarcated; hence the disputes which arose. The determination of the borders became unavoidable; otherwise, a state of flux with constant advance and retreat northward and southward would continue indefinitely.

Only if we bear in mind the area's strategic significance, the importance of the wells, the distribution of and the divisions between the various tribes and, above all, the desire of the mandating state to minimize trouble and provide a measure of stability can we visualize the true magnitude of these border problems, the form they took and their intractability.

In Chapter 1, the various steps in the development of the Sultanate of Najd and its Dependencies were outlined in order to trace how the border problems emerged, how varied they were and how intractable they proved to be. Chapter 2 has taken up this same theme and discussed the emergence of one new state in Iraq and another in Transjordan. Both of these were carved out of the Ottoman Empire and placed under British mandate, which, as has been made abundantly clear in the foregoing, was just a mask. The following chapter will analyse the relations of the Sultanate of Najd with its neighbours, and the position adopted by both the Ottoman Empire and Britain towards this new state.

3
The Relations of the Sultanate of Najd with its Neighbours

Relations with Hejaz, Transjordan and Iraq

In the light of the foregoing discussion, it is clear that relations between Najd and Hejaz—or, to put it differently, relations between Imam Sultan Abdul-Aziz and Sherif Hussein—were formed as a result of a number of factors, including Hussein's ambition to become the King of the Arabs and to be the head of an Arab state which included the Arabian peninsula. Such aspirations were not consistent with the establishment, growth and expansion of the Sultanate of Najd, and conflicted with the Arab, Islamic and international position which King Abdul-Aziz had come to occupy.

As mentioned above, the capture by Najd of Hā'il and the entire north up to al-Jof, Sakaka and Wādī al-Sarhan, and then the annexation of 'Asīr, clearly indicated that Hejaz would be next.[1] Added to this was the fact that the tribes in the border areas were linked in one way or another to both Najd and Hejaz. However, the relations of Najd with Hejaz were significantly affected by differences over determining the border which separated the two areas.[2]

At the time, Hejaz did not have established borders, although the Arabs referred to Jabal al-Surat, which separates Najd from Tihama, as such a border. The name 'Hejaz' has been used ever since the flourishing of international trade along the various land and sea routes, thus making the mountain chain more accessible to trade caravans. Etymologically, Hejaz acquired its name because it was 'trapped' (in Arabic: *ihtajāza*) by the mountains, or because it acted as a 'buffer' (in Arabic: *hājiz*) between Najd and Tihama, as in fact there was such a buffer which extended from Yemen almost to al-Shām.[3]

For the ancient geographers, Hejaz stood for the Sarawat mountain chain, extending from Yemen almost to al-Shām, which acted as a buffer between Najd and Tihama: what flows down the western slopes must land in Tihama, and what flows down the eastern slopes must land in Najd. Hejaz was a mountain which stood between the depression of Tihama and Najd. Just as it prevented one from mingling with the other, Hejaz was also a buffer. The reference was extended to include Mecca, Jiddah, al-Madīnah, Yanbu' and al-Laith together with the surrounding areas.[4]

In the area which separates Najd and Hejaz stands al-Bityila, a black, pyramid-shaped mountain east of al-Hidn. Beyond al-Bityila and below al-Hidn stands another black mountain—al-Buraim, which can be seen from the nearby road as if it were hanging from on high. Parallel to al-Bityila and al-Buraim stands the famous giant mountain al-Hidn, blocking the horizon and extending from east to west, with its peaks high in the sky overlooking Turba and al-Kharma. This mountain has become proverbial among the Arabs for its extensive flanks and vastness. Al-Hidn acquired its name in ancient times. In *Mu'jam al-Buldan*, Yaqut describes it as the first of Najd's borders. There is a proverbial saying, 'Whoever sees al-Hidn is in Najd and whatever is behind him is in Tihama.'[5]

Sherif Hussein considered Turba and al-Kharma to be Hejazi villages, separated from Najd by the desert. Imam Abdul-Aziz, on the other hand, felt that they were Najdi, as al-Hidn mountain constitutes a natural barrier separating Najd and Hejaz.[6] Every time they mentioned punishing the rebels, Sherif Hussein and his son Abdullah were referring to the two desert lands of Turba and al-Kharma.

Sherif Hussein persisted in inciting trouble in the areas surrounding Najd. He started by supplying the Emirs of Hā'il with funds and arms. (That was before the great defeat which they suffered, as explained in Chapter 1 above.) Hussein also sent funds and a military force to the 'Ayid Emirs, who eventually met a fate similar to those of Hā'il, with their capital—Abha—becoming one of Najd's dependencies.

The clash between Najd and Sherif Hussein eventually took place in a series of battles. The Najdi forces engaged the Sherifian army at Turba and al-Kharma, dealing them a severe blow and utterly defeating them. Imam Abdul-Aziz's prudence always ensured that his own armies came back victorious.[7] Sherif Hussein could do nothing further against the people of Najd except prevent them from performing the *haj* (pilgrimage). This was very serious. Since the people of Najd were followers of the Salafi call, they could not possibly suspend the observance of the *haj*, one of the pillars of Islam. Furthermore, the Sherif constantly incited the bedouin to harass the inhabitants of Turba and al-Kharma.[8]

Sherif Hussein was so keen to gain control of the border areas east of Hejaz that he himself led some of the campaigns against the 'Utaiba in Najd. The 'Utaiba comprised a group of tribes, the majority of whom were from Hawazin, and whose homelands extended from the Hejaz border to al-Washm land in Najd and the Qasīm desert in the north-east.[9]

In the battle of Turbat Sha'ban in 1918, however, at which the Sherifian army was defeated, the magnitude of the catastrophe and the size of the losses devastated Sherif Hussein. The entire Hejaz seemed to be on the verge of falling into the hands of Imam Abdul-Aziz. In addition to considering Turba and al-Kharma as parts of Hejaz, Hussein feared for Turba which was on the road to Taif: while Turba is on the trade route between Hejaz and Najd, it is the gateway to Taif from the Najdi side and to the fortress of Taif from the Hejazi side.

Although the Emirs of al-Kharma were from the Lu'ai family, who were 'Abadila dignitaries, they tended to be more loyal to the Al Saud, a loyalty which went back to the era of the Great Imam Muhammad bin Saud. They had been influenced by the call for unity and reform and had thus responded to the call of Sheikh Muhammad bin Abdul-Wahab, maintaining good relations with the Saudi state ever since. Although Khalid bin Lu'ai, the Emir of al-Kharma, took it upon himself to mediate between Sherif Hussein and Imam Abdul-Aziz, Ibn Lu'ai finally sided with the Imam.[10]

Neither Turba nor al-Kharma were economically significant except for being close to the two important trade routes which link the middle of the Arabian peninsula with Mecca and further on with the Red Sea. The first of these routes starts at Riyadh and the second at Buraida, the base of the Qasīm region, linking up with Kuwait on the coast of the Arabian Gulf. This area is thus considered the main outlet from Najd, and the key to Hejaz. But it is no more than this, as far as the economic advantages were concerned.[11]

In the light of the various developments outlined above, however, Turba and al-Kharma assumed far more importance from another angle. Each of these two areas came to be seen as a symbol for the real leadership of the Arabian peninsula. The bid for such a leadership had moved from the arena of Qasīm and Shammar to the borders of Hejaz.[12] As we have seen, Najd actually made such a bid on the borders between Najd and Hejaz, and Najdi leadership of the Arabian peninsula seemed assured.[13]

Sherif Hussein's last resort was to contact his British allies. Britain sent Imam Sultan Abdul-Aziz a notification which read as follows: 'His Majesty's government requests that you return to Najd and leave Turba and al-Kharma free and uncontrolled until peace is concluded and the borders determined....'[14]

In the period following Sherif Hussein's declaration of his revolt against the Ottomans and his attempt to gain the Caliphate, and because of the deteriorating situation in which he found himself, Imam Abdul-Aziz invited the Sherif to negotiate the precise borders between Najd and Hejaz, 'in order to remove doubt and redouble the assistance to the people of Najd'.

But Sherif Hussein misread Najdi assistance as an endorsement of his desired status as King of all the Arabs; he felt that the leadership of the Arabian peninsula, and indeed the prospective Caliphate over all Muslims, were destined to be his. As has already been shown, this was not borne out by the facts; reality led in a totally different direction.

When the First World War ended, and the Turkish garrison in al-Madīnah succumbed to Emir Abdullah bin Hussein, Imam Abdul-Aziz invited Sherif Hussein once again to discuss the border issue and the question of the tribes who shared the area between Najd and Hejaz.[15] But instead of responding positively to these repeated invitations, Sherif Hussein instructed his son Emir Abdullah to write to all the Arab leaders informing them that the fighting around al-Madīnah had ended. Emir Abdullah also wrote to Imam Abdul-Aziz, telling him that, as the situation stood, the government of his father Sherif Hussein now had nothing to distract it from attending to the internal affairs of Hejaz, and inflicting an exemplary punishment on those tribes who were intent on causing damage and subversion. This was a specific reference to Turba and al-Kharma, and Hussein's determination to exercise control over the area between Hejaz and Najd.[16] This was followed by a ban on Najdis performing the *haj* until Najd withdrew from al-Jof, Turba and al-Kharma.[17]

Before moving on to discuss Najd's relations with Iraq, it may be useful at this stage to indicate the kind of border problems which existed between Kuwait and the Sultanate of Najd and its Dependencies. The raids of the Mutair tribe on areas of Kuwait led to tension in the relations between the two countries. Of all the raids, we may single out the one which took place in 1919 and which led to the battle of Homs. This forced the Emir of Kuwait to build a wall round the city as a defence, and consequently to raise the tax on pearl-traders, driving most of them out of Kuwait.

In the following year, Feisal al-Dawish renewed his attacks on al-Jahra' in Kuwait. British planes took part in chasing his men away and dropped leaflets informing them that they must withdraw from the land.[18] Nevertheless, Imam Abdul-Aziz persisted in issuing categorical orders that people were not to engage in aggressive acts against their neighbours, that attacks were not to be launched without his explicit permission and that anyone who contravened these orders would be executed.[19]

The new states in the region were in uproar concerning the instability of the surrounding areas. But Imam Abdul-Aziz felt that these problems could be solved by ensuring that the desert and settled lands of neighbouring states were closed to fugitive insurgents, a policy which could only be achieved by Iraq and Transjordan's undertaking to hand over those who sought refuge in their countries.[20]

Hence, the border agreement between Najd and Kuwait came into being, stipulating that the Najd–Kuwait western border began from the Wādī al-'Uja junction and that al-Ruq'a belonged to Najd. From that point, the border would extend in a straight line until it met the twenty-ninth parallel. This line was to continue until it terminated at a point on the coast, south of Ra's al-Qulai'a, which was to be the southern border. The area common to both Najd and Kuwait had this line as its northern border, a rib of land called al-Shiq as its western border and the sea as its eastern border. As its southern border, this area had a line which in the west passes by the east of al-Shiq until 'Ain al-'Id, and then on to the coast to the north up to Ra's al-Mish'ab. Both Kuwait and Najd were to have equal rights to this area, pending a further agreement, endorsed by Britain, to determine its status.[21]

In 1922 a conference was held in al-Muhammara, attended by representatives of Imam Abdul-Aziz and of the governments of Iraq and Britain, to look into issues relating to the borders and the clans in areas between Najd and Iraq. The stance adopted by Imam Abdul-Aziz at this conference was basically that in occupying Najd, al-Ihsā' and al-Qasīm he was merely regaining what was his, his father's and his forefathers'; that the Dhufair tribe in Iraq were subjects of the Al Saud; that al-'Amarat and al-Rola were actually from 'Anza; and that Banu al-Hathal and al-Sha'lan were also Saudi subjects.

As the Imam had in fact already retaken Jabal Shammar, he had the right to reclaim the tribes and clans which had run away from the Jabal and sought refuge in neighbouring countries.[22] Delegates to this conference signed the Muhammara agreement. Although the Imam did not at first agree to it, a few months later, while signing two protocols in al-'Uqair, he did agree to put his signature to it. The text of this agreement follows.

Article 1

a. The clans of al-Muntafik, al-Dhufair and al-'Amarat shall return to the government of Iraq. The governments of Iraq and Najd shall agree mutually to prevent the transgressions of the clans of one party on the territories of the other, and to punish the transgressors.

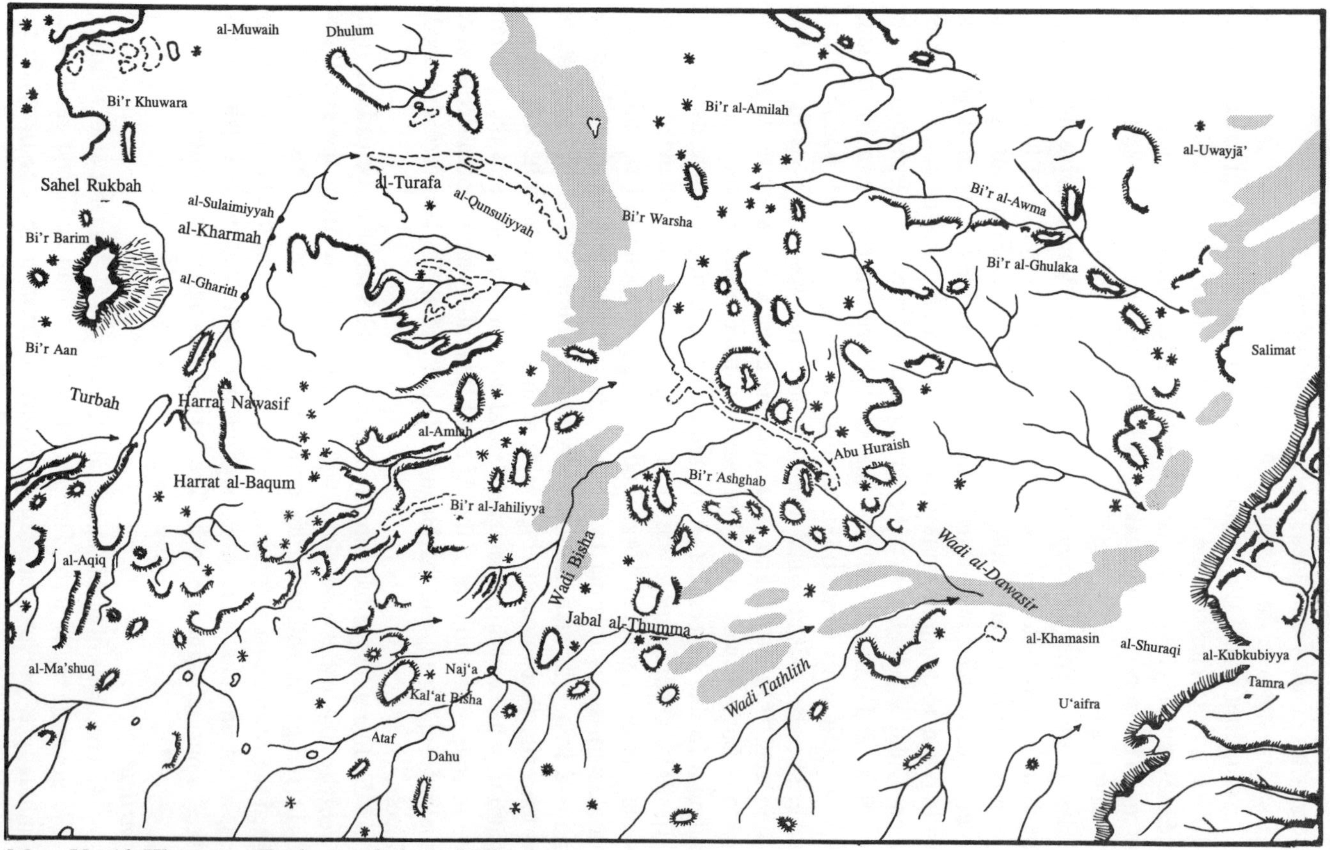

Map V. Al-Kharma, Turba and their Villages

b. In accordance with the objection raised by the representative of the Najdi government regarding the nature of the borders suggested by the representative of Iraq, the following was agreed:

In accordance with resolution (a), the clans of al-Muntafik, al-Dhufair and al-'Amarat shall return to Iraq and the Shammar of Najd to Najd. The wells and lands which have always been used by the clans of Iraq are to return to Iraq, and those which have always been used by the Shammar of Najd to Najd. To determine these wells and lands, and demarcate the borders[23] on this basis, agreement has been reached to establish a committee consisting of two experts from each state, and presided over by an official from the British government to be selected by the British High Commissioner. The committee is to meet in Baghdad, with the parties concerned accepting without objection its decisions regarding the absolute demarcation of borders.

Article II

The government of Iraq and the government of Najd undertake to secure the pilgrimage route and, each within its own borders, to protect individual pilgrims from any act of aggression.

Article III

a. The two governments agree that all commercial transactions shall be safe from any acts of aggression.

b. Natural and manufactured products imported by Iraq from Najd, and those exported to Najd, shall be subject to the same treatment accorded to those products of other friendly countries with regard to import, export and transit taxes.

Article IV

The two governments agree to freedom of movement within their territories for the purposes of trade and commerce, provided that the appropriate documentation is in hand.

Article V

The clans of each party, when selling in the lands of the other party, shall be subject to the appropriate taxes.

In an appendix to this treaty, paragraph 2 reads as follows:

The representative of the Najd government undertakes that until the decision of the committee which shall meet in Baghdad, no act of aggression shall emanate from the Najdi clans against the clans of Iraq.[24]

The 'Uqair protocol no. 1 is an annexe to the Muhammara agreement. This protocol consists of the following clauses:

Article I

a. The eastern border shall commence from the bed of Wādī al-'Uja. From this point, the border of the Najdi Kingdom shall begin, extending in a straight line to a well called al-Waqba in Turk al-Dulaimiyya and al-Waqba north of this line and from al-Waqba it shall extend north-west to Bir Ansab.

b. Beginning at the above-mentioned point, the borders of Iraq shall extend in a straight line to the north-west of al-Amghar. From there, the line shall extend south-west in a straight line until it reaches the border of Najd from Bir Ansab.

Article II

Since many of the wells are now within the Iraqi borders, with the Najdi side thus deprived of them, the Iraqi government undertakes not to debar the clans of the Najdi Kingdom settled on the edge of the borders from using the neighbouring wells in the Iraqi territories if these wells are nearer than those within the Najdi borders.

Article III

The two governments undertake not to use the waters or wells on the edge of each other's borders for any military purpose such as the building of fortifications or the mobilization of soldiers.

The 'Uqair protocol no. 2 stipulates that:

> Since the government of Iraq and the government of Najd have agreed to the demarcation of the borders between them, the two governments undertake not to stand in the way of any clan or branch of a clan which is outside the borders of either party and which is not affiliated to either government, if this clan or branch of a clan have aligned themselves and opted to be under the jurisdiction of either government.[25]

Nevertheless, objections were raised in certain quarters—most prominently by Feisal al-Dawish and those who joined in from the 'Ajman tribe—to allowing the clans of Transjordan and Iraq to graze in the lands of Najd and its Dependencies, a measure which they viewed as abominable.

Although this issue outlived the Kuwait Conference, it nevertheless sheds light on how difficult it was to settle the border disputes, particularly at the edge of desert lands. Imam Abdul-Aziz consequently felt that he had to call the Riyadh Conference early in 1927, at which he made clear his adherence to the Shari'a. At the end of the conference, the *ulema* of Najd issued a *fatwa* rebutting the claims of the Ikhwan (the religious brotherhood of the Wahabi sect), and enjoining them not to engage in a *jihad* unless Imam Abdul-Aziz ruled that this was in the best interests of all Muslims.[26]

At another meeting two years later, a number of delegates addressed Imam Abdul-Aziz, saying:

> You know that the entire desert belongs to us, the people of Najd, and you remember our objection to granting them borders in this desert unjustly, as we are free to graze anywhere we like in this desert. You then informed us that, in accordance with the treaty you signed at al-'Uqair, they are allowed neither to erect buildings in these lands, nor establish camps round either the wells or the waters.

The rebels' response to the Imam's statements and the *ulema*'s *fatwa*, however, was to persist in their raids on the Iraqi borders. Relations thus came to focus on negotiations regarding the demarcation of borders, in which the British side (which had been seconded to Iraq) took part. It should be noted here that the *hijar* represented the most decisive measure in dealing with this problem.[27]

As far as Najd's relations with Transjordan are concerned, we may here note the factors which shaped them and which have been discussed earlier in terms of the annexation by Najd of Wādī al-Sarhan and its capital, al-Jof.

Sultan Abdul-Aziz saw the need to find a direct point of contact with Syria. This would enable the Salafi call to spread northward. Britain, under whose mandate Transjordan was administered, however, was seeking to annex this area to Transjordan.[28]

The area northwest of Hā'il was awash with Shammar tribes who came to graze. This area, which extended like a corner into Transjordan, constituted a weak link in the belt which the British sought to consolidate north of the emerging Sultanate of Najd and its Dependencies. Thus, when Imam Abdul-Aziz's forces embarked on the liberation of this area, the Imam anxiously awaited Britain's reaction.[29]

Once again, Ikhwan forces pushed into al-Jof some 50 kilometres inside the Emirate of Transjordan. As mentioned above, al-Jof was an important trade centre through which the caravans passed on their way from Baghdad to Egypt. Whichever power occupied this oasis would threaten Palestine and

Transjordan, with the balance of power turning in its favour. On another occasion, a group of the Ikhwan penetrated nearly 100 kilometres into the desert, right over the Transjordanian border, and reached the village of Turaif, 80 kilometres from Amman, the new capital of Transjordan.

It can thus be seen that the border problems between Najd and Hejaz, Iraq and Transjordan had still not been solved. As has been made clear, these problems focused on: the demarcation of the actual borders; the distribution of the clans and tribes and their various branches; grazing lands, wells and water; control of the tribes and preventing acts of aggression; and, finally, the desire of the various parties to take possession of areas of strategic and economic importance.

The Position vis-à-vis *the Ottoman Empire*

In this review of Najd's relations with its neighbours, two further issues demand examination: first, the position of the Ottoman Empire regarding the regaining of Riyadh up to the start of the First World War; and, second, Britain's position regarding the regaining of Riyadh until the end of the period addressed in this book. The latter is particularly important for its close links with the Kuwait Conference.

As the Ottoman Empire was the great Islamic power, established in the name of and for Islam, whose Sultans enjoyed the title of Caliph, the Ottoman leaders made a bid for the undisputed leadership of the Muslim world in order to face the Christian West. When Mamluk rule ended, the task of protecting the holy shrines was transferred to the Ottoman Sultans, who succeeded in becoming the leading power in the Islamic world, although they failed to dominate the Persians.

The Arabian peninsula became the most important part of the Empire. The Arab territories were also particularly significant for the Ottomans. Hejaz was of paramount importance, for within it were the holy shrines.[30] Thus, the survival and name of the Ottoman Empire, as well as the title of its Sultans, came to be inextricably linked with the survival of the Arab lands, particularly Hejaz, as its constituent parts. We have seen how the Ottomans resisted al-Dar'iyya in the reign of the first Saudi state, and how they repeatedly attempted to bring down al-Dar'iyya, either by inciting the *wālis* of al-Shām, Baghdad and Hejaz, or by inciting the tribes and *al-Ashrāf* and eventually by sending in Muhammad Ali and his brutal army to destroy al-Dar'iyya as the base of the call for unity and reform.

Ever since the days of the first Saudi state, the Al Saud have carried the title of Imam because they established their state on the correct basis of

Islam and the Salafi call, at a time when the Ottoman Empire and its people had deviated from the correct Islamic path. In fact, for the Saudi state, the title Imam came to symbolize their lack of dependence on the Ottomans.[31]

Ottoman policy was therefore one of opposition to the establishment of the Saudi state. This attitude began during the reign of the ancestors of King Abdul-Aziz. The battles of some of the Ottoman *wālis* in Hejaz, Iraq and Egypt with the people of Najd are well known. But the most important reason for these differences is that the Saudis did not endorse the Ottoman Caliphate; and that ever since Sheikh Muhammad bin Abdul-Wahab had issued his reformist call, the people of Najd had made public their allegiance to the leadership of the Al Saud, who were the Imams in charge of them. Furthermore, the Najdi lands had always been loath to succumb to the Ottoman Sultans. This explains why, when the Rashīds—who were pro-Ottoman and loyal to the Ottoman Caliphate—rose in opposition, they were adopted by the Ottomans as their main support in the Arabian peninsula.[32]

When Ibn Rashīd took Riyadh and Imam Abdul-Rahman al-Feisal left for al-Hasa, which was in the hands of the Ottomans, 'Akif Pasha, the *mutassarif* of al-Hasa, welcomed Abdul-Rahman and requested him, in the name of the Ottoman government, to co-operate in regaining Riyadh, on condition that, in return for arms and protection, he recognize Ottoman sovereignty. But Imam Abdul-Rahman declined, as this ran counter to the principles of the Salafi state, and because he scorned the idea of living under a state which he had always considered to have no right to be in his country. Shortly after this, Imam Abdul-Rahman left for Kuwait.[33]

With Imam Abdul-Aziz's rapid seizure of Riyadh and control of Najd, he came to represent a threat to the Ottoman Empire. The Turks feared he might resurrect the Salafi movement, which had previously cost them dearly. They also saw the increase in his strength and influence as a factor which could cost them their dominance and position in the area. The Ottomans' status in the Arab territories was by this time unclear, particularly with Kuwait's becoming a British protectorate, the Yemen revolt's flaring up and the rebels proclaiming Imam Yahya as leader in 1904, and the widespread civil strife in Basra.[34] In an attempt to reverse these trends, the Turks gave unequivocal support to the Rashīds as a reward for their recognition of the Ottoman Caliphate, and decided to use them as a power base in the Arabian peninsula against the newly emerging power in Najd.

When the Rashīds warned that Imam Abdul-Aziz was becoming increasingly powerful and influential, the Ottomans took the warning seriously and wrote to Imam Abdul-Rahman al-Feisal, requesting him to prevent his son from engaging in military operations against the Rashīds. The Ottomans also instructed their men and garrisons in al-Hasa, before it was annexed by Imam Abdul-Aziz, to watch Abdul-Aziz's movements and prevent him from entering the towns and villages of al-Hasa and procuring what he needed from those markets.[35]

In a separate development, the Ottomans were quick to prop up Ibn Rashīd and supply him with funds, men and arms. However, because of the successive defeats of the Rashīds, particularly at the battle of Shattana in 1904, which is considered a decisive event in the history of Najd, the Turks were forced to change their policy. The battle of Rawdat Muhana followed in 1906, ending with the death of Abdul-Aziz bin Mit'ib bin Abdullah bin Rashīd.[36]

Numerous conferences and rounds of negotiations followed. First came the Basra Conference between Imam Abdul-Rahman and Fakhri Pasha, the *wāli* of Basra, and then the 'Unaiza Conference between Abdul-Rahman and Ahmad Faidi Pasha. The latter conference resumed the business of the Basra Conference, with Faidi Pasha as leader of the Ottoman expeditionary force which left Basra and headed for Buraida to terrorize Najd. However, Faidi Pasha was forced to negotiate instead. The Ottomans' change of policy, in opting for negotiations and attempting to reach an understanding with Najd, enfuriated the Rashīds and shook their confidence in the Empire.[37]

The Ottomans were alarmed by the successive victories of Imam Abdul-Aziz. Their policies had been utterly ineffective in the Arabian peninsula and, in the aftermath of the repeated defeats of the Rashīds, the Ottomans realized that the door was now wide open for Najd to move into Hā'il.

Dissatisfied with the apathy and inaction of their resident Commander in al-Qasīm, Sidqī Pasha, the Ottomans dispatched Sami Pasha al-Faruqi from al-Madīnah to make contact with Ibn Rashīd. Al-Faruqi was of Arab origin. He agreed with the Rashīds that an attempt should be made to convince Imam Abdul-Aziz that al-Qasīm should be under Ottoman control—in other words, it should be a buffer zone between Najd and Jabal Shammar—and that the Ottomans should establish a military command centre in both 'Unaiza and Buraida. Al-Faruqi then arrived at al-Shihiyya, which is west of Buraida and north of al-Bakiriyya, and requested a meeting with Imam Abdul-Aziz. They met at al-Bakiriyya, but the Imam categorically rejected every proposal put forward by al-Faruqi.[38]

While still in al-Bakiriyya, the Imam sent al-Faruqi a message giving him a choice between: (a) withdrawing his army to al-Sirr within five days; (b) avoiding any contact with the Rashīds; and (c) Abdul-Aziz's taking it upon himself to remove the army from the area, sending the Iraqis who came with Faidi Pasha back to Iraq, and the Shāmis who came with Sidqī Pasha back to al-Madīnah. Failing this, the Imam warned, war was inevitable.

Al-Faruqi reluctantly accepted the latter option. The Ottomans sent a message thanking Imam Abdul-Aziz, 'the historic Emir and the great leader, Abdul-Aziz Pasha Saud', for his honourable treatment of their troops.[39]

As previously mentioned, relations between the Turks and the Arabs in general had developed in such a way that for the Arabs to align themselves with the Ottoman Empire at the start of the First World War was no longer a proposition that attracted unanimous approval. This, however, does not in any way justify Sherif Hussein's inclination to side with the other camp, that is, with Britain and the other Allies, during the war. All this created a climate in which the independent and strictly neutral position adopted by the Sultanate of Najd and its Dependencies was shown to be the best policy.

When the war broke out, the Sherif of Mecca, Hussein bin Ali, received two letters informing him that the Ottoman Empire had entered the war on the side of Germany and Austro-Hungary. The first letter was from the Ottoman Sultan, Muhammad V. It included the writ declaring a *jihad* and an invitation to Sherif Hussein to declare a *jihad* too, in his capacity as Custodian of the Two Holy Shrines. The second letter was from the Commander of the Fourth Ottoman Army, Lieutenant-General Jamal Pasha, Governor-General of Syria and Lebanon. The Commander called upon Sherif Hussein to send him the honourable flag of the Prophet from al-Madīnah to Damascus, to be flown on high leading the way to Suez.[40] Jamal Pasha was one of the leading Unionists. During the war he was given absolute powers to govern Greater Syria, and it was he who imposed numerous death sentences under the pretext of possessing documents from the French Consulate implicating a number of Arab personalities.[41]

At the same time that Sherif Hussein wrote to Lord Kitchener stating that he was on the side of the Allies in the war and expressing his readiness to declare the Arab revolt against the Ottomans, the Sherif wrote to the Ottoman Sultan and Jamal Pasha, expressing his ardent enthusiasm for the declaration of a *jihad*. There was the proviso, however, that he could not make public his positive stance towards the Ottoman Empire because one British fleet was stationed in the Arabian Gulf and controlled the entire coastal area, and another British fleet was in the Red Sea.

An Ottoman delegation arrived from al-Madīnah including Muhammad Shukri al-Alusi. The delegation tried to curry favour with Imam Abdul-Aziz, begging him to side with the Ottomans.[42] But how could any alignment be conceivable, given the circumstances, developments and implications referred to above and which came to govern the relations of the Arabs with the Ottoman Empire? Furthermore, what was the value of an alignment with a regime which had been suffering from internal unrest and ideological chaos since the beginning of the nineteenth century, a regime that had changed from reform to secularism (Tanzimat) and finally to Turanian nationalism, only to move from a stage of stagnation to that of weakness and collapse?

What was the value of an alignment with a regime that had become the traditional enemy of the call to unity and reform and of the Al Saud, who stood for supporting this call and spreading the Salafi doctrine? If the Sherifian regime in Hejaz had previously assisted this regime to tarnish the Salafi call, this regime now stood as one of its opponents, while the Al Saud honourably adhered to neutrality.[43]

It was as if the Ottoman stance had manifested itself in traditional policies bent on opposing the establishment of a Salafi Saudi state. The Ottomans implemented this policy through traditional means, inciting their *wālis* in al-Shām and Iraq, instigating the Sherifian regime in Hejaz and stirring up the tribes in the areas which were under its control. The Ottomans also used the Emirate of the Rashīds in the mountains as a tool to achieve their ends. This often took the form of outright war, as has been shown above.

This situation in the north of the peninsula, and on the borders of Najd nearby, had repercussions on the tribes which traditionally raided, attacked and then withdrew. These areas could now be described as volatile. This was later to create serious difficulties in the demarcation of the borders. The most acute of these problems was the attempt to enforce this demarcation, that is, to persuade the tribes to recognize and adhere to it.

The period of the First World War can be seen as one of military confrontation between the Ottoman Empire and a part of the Arab nation, on the one hand, and Hejaz and al-Shām, on the other. The confrontation was aided and led by the British. In fact, in the beginning, it seemed as though the Turkish forces were fighting the Arabs more than the Allied forces.[44]

The Ottoman Empire lost the First World War and thereby all the Arab territories. But those Arab forces which joined the Allies in this war were losers too, failing to realize their own hopes or what had been promised them by the Allies. Sherif Hussein not only had his hopes dashed, but also lost his position in the Islamic world. It became abundantly clear that the Sultanate of Najd and its Dependencies was the only hope left for the Arabian peninsula, for pan-Arabism and for Islam.

In discussing the position *vis-à-vis* the Ottoman Empire, we began by underlining the importance of the Arabian peninsula as a whole to the Turks. Hejaz was particularly important because it was the basic factor in shaping the recent history of the relations between the various forces in the Arab region.

The Relations of the Sultanate of Najd with its Neighbours

The Position vis-à-vis *Britain*

We shall approach the position *vis-à-vis* Britain in the same way, pointing out the strategic significance of the Arabian peninsula for Britain also. This was a basic factor in the shaping of the history of international relations in the Arab world.

India was the largest and most important British colony and the biggest market for British industrial goods. India was the cornerstone of the British Empire and of a continental regime extending from Aden to Hong Kong. Thus, the British Government of India played an important role in the affairs of its neighbours. This meant that Britain adopted a policy of 'securing' India. The British explained this concept in terms of India's being a 'fruit', the core of all the other colonies, which should therefore be covered by a protective shell. This protection was to consist of Iran, the Arabian peninsula and the vast expanse of desert from Baghdad to Damascus. In addition, Britain wanted to secure what it called the Empire route, which extended from India to the Mediterranean through the Arabian Gulf and the Red Sea. Britain consequently adopted a step-by-step policy throughout the nineteenth century, with the aim of controlling the Arabian Gulf and the Red Sea.[45]

The East India Company—established in the late sixteenth century at the end of the reign of Elizabeth I—also played a vital role in implementing Britain's strategy in the Arabian Gulf region. It was the company which shouldered the responsibilities of colonizing India and dominating the Indian Ocean and the Arabian Gulf, and, in collaboration with the Levant Company, it established what came to be known as the Empire route.

The East India Company saw to it that this task was carried out until the mid-nineteenth century. Placed under its authority were the Government of India and the Residency in Bombay which looked after British interests in the region, the Indian Navy, the British Resident Representative in the Gulf and his deputy in Baghdad, and the British Resident Representative in Aden.

In the mid-nineteenth century, Britain established the India Office, with a Secretary of State for Indian Affairs, under whose authority were placed all the bodies listed above which had previously been under the authority of the East India Company. In other words, direct supervision was transferred from the company to the British government.

It was the East India Company with its various bodies which, afraid that British influence in the Arabian Gulf might decline, was particularly alarmed by the establishment of the first Saudi state, as this became a Gulf state with the seizure of al-Hasa, Oman, Qatar and Bahrain. The East India Company also tried to exert a measure of control over the Emirs, Sheikhs and Sultans of the eastern coast of the Arabian peninsula through protection treaties.

When Muhammad Ali captured al-Dar'iyya, thus replacing Britain in supervising the Arabian Gulf, Britain contrived a plan which destroyed his control in the entire Arabian peninsula, in accordance with the resolutions of the London Conference of 1840. Britain's policy was to concentrate on consolidating its influence on the coast of the Arabian peninsula, avoiding as far as possible any confrontation with forces in the interior of the peninsula, and controlling points of access to the Gulf. This explains why Britain sought to conclude an early agreement with Sheikh Mubarak al-Sabah on 22 January 1899 which Malcolm John Meade, the British Resident Representative in the Gulf, signed and which was modelled on other kinds of protection treaties. This agreement stipulated that the Sheikh was to receive no representative of any other state, and that he was to concede, sell, mortgage or rent no land without the prior consent of the British government.

This was followed by the visit of Lord Curzon, the Viceroy of India, to Kuwait in 1904, when he reached an agreement concerning the appointment of Colonel Knox as the first British Representative in Kuwait. Knox was accompanied by Lord Hardinge, the Viceroy of India, on his visit to Kuwait in 1914 to sound out the Kuwaitis regarding the First World War.[46]

Britain felt that its colonial activity in the Arabian Gulf, at its point of entry, in Kuwait, and along the western coast, was an integral part of its colonial activity in Egypt and Sudan and its control of the Suez Canal. It also saw that the route through the Gulf, connecting to the land route from Kuwait to Iraq and on to the Mediterranean coast, was the best mail route. Given all this, Britain decided to consolidate its influence and speedily declared Kuwait a protectorate. The Ottomans were watching this struggle for influence with the utmost concern, which led to the Grand Vizier's accepting the German proposals for the establishment of the Berlin–Baghdad railway. Britain saw this measure as an expression of German supremacy in the affairs of the Ottoman Empire, and a serious threat to its own Empire route through the Arabian Gulf.

When Imam Abdul-Aziz succeeded in regaining Riyadh, Britain began to turn its attention to the relationship with Najd, calling on the assistance of Sheikh Mubarak, the ruler of Kuwait.[47] The struggle over Kuwait was complex. As we have seen, Britain declared Kuwait a protectorate. The Ottomans, on the other hand, sought to achieve this very aim by inciting the Rashīds on more than one occasion, but they were to be repeatedly rebuffed and forced to retreat by the British warships patrolling the Gulf.

In 1911 Captain Shakespear, the British Political Agent in Kuwait, managed to secure an audience with Imam Abdul-Aziz. This was the first time that a British official had had the honour of meeting the Imam. As mentioned above, Britain had followed a policy of interference in the affairs of the Arabian peninsula only in so far as this served to secure its route through the Gulf. Britain had also been committed to non-interference in bedouin affairs. However, Ottoman activity in the Gulf, and the plan to establish a railway to reach the head of the Gulf with German assistance, led Britain to change its policy.[48]

When Imam Abdul-Aziz regained al-Hasa and thus acquired a base overlooking the Arabian Gulf, with Najd becoming a Gulf state, the Ottomans, reeling under successive defeats in western Tripoli and the Balkans, approached the Imam and offered their endorsement of his annexation of al-Hasa to Najd. They also accepted that al-Hasa and Najd become one *vilayet* under their own jurisdiction, appointing Imam Abdul-Aziz as its *wāli*.

Britain then hastened to occupy Basra in 1914, which meant that Britain now dominated the Gulf. From Basra, Britain advanced towards the point at which the Tigris meets the Euphrates, forming the Shatt al-Arab. Britain was thus able to impose an economic blockade round the coasts of al-Hasa.[49]

Britain then demanded, through its Foreign Secretary, Sir Edward Grey, that negotiations begin with the Turkish ambassador to London, Ibrahim Haqqi Pasha, to clarify the position of each of the two parties in the areas adjacent to the Gulf. These negotiations, which took place in the summer of 1913, dealt with the situation regarding Kuwait, Bahrain and the neutral coastal Emirates. However, the position concerning al-Hasa was not broached. The negotiations went on for three months but the agreement was not to be ratified until months later.

In this agreement, Britain managed to snatch away from the Ottoman Empire the right to consolidate its influence in all the countries of southern Arabia, south of the line which begins from the Qatar peninsula and extends southward to the extreme west of the border agreed on between the protectorate of Aden and the Ottoman *vilayet* of Yemen.[50] Among the reasons which led Britain to adopt such measures was the arrival just before the First World War of a French envoy offering vast annual financial assistance from France in return for the Ottomans securing the French trade in arms at al-'Uqair and al-Qatīf. The overall aim was to use the situation to counteract Britain's influence and trade monopoly in the Gulf.[51]

As mentioned earlier, on his visit to Kuwait in 1914, Lord Hardinge had called for the convening of a conference in Kuwait to be attended by the son of Bahrain's ruler, the ruler of Arabistan, the Sultan of Oman and the Sultan of Najd to discuss the consequences if the Ottomans decided to enter the war. This conference, however, did not achieve the necessary quorum to function.[52] Imam Abdul-Aziz was preoccupied with the battle of Jarab[53] against Saud bin Abdul-Aziz bin Mit'ib bin Rashīd.

By this time, Najd's trade had come almost to a standstill along with that of the rest of the Ottoman territories: Ibn Rashīd was in the north, Sherif Hussein was in the west, Basra was occupied by Britain and Kuwait had become a British protectorate. The only outlet for Najd was the Gulf coast. The fighting between Najd and Ibn Rashīd which took place in 1915 ended in stalemate; the situation was aggravated by the rebellion of the 'Ajman, the most important tribe in al-Hasa. In the midst of all this, Britain sent out Sir Percy Cox, its Political Resident in the Gulf. In the Saudi port of al-'Uqair, a treaty was signed[54] which included the following among its articles:

> 1. The British government shall recognize and endorse that Najd, al-Hasa, al-Qatīf and al-Jubail and the Dependencies are lands belonging to Ibn Saud and his ancestors before him, and that Ibn Saud is therefore an independent ruler of these lands and an absolute chief of their tribes.
>
> ....
>
> 5. Ibn Saud shall undertake to provide within his territories freedom of passage on all the routes leading to the holy places, and to protect pilgrims going to and returning from these places.
>
> 6. Ibn Saud...shall undertake to refrain from aggression against the countries of Kuwait, Bahrain, the Qatar Sheikhdoms and the coasts of Oman which are under British protection. The borders of these countries shall be determined in due course.
>
> 7. The British government and Ibn Saud agree to the conclusion of a treaty[55] that is more detailed regarding matters of mutual interest to the two parties.[56]

When the First World War broke out, what the British feared most was that the Turks might establish an Arab front which blocked the route to India: hence the meetings at al-'Uqair, al-Qatīf and Darin Island. The British also managed to conclude the 1915 treaty referred to above. Sir Percy Cox was trying to sound out Imam Abdul-Aziz before Britain embarked on an agreement with Sherif Hussein.

The Ottoman Empire's joining the Central Powers against the Allies was an important factor in revitalizing British political moves. But British diplomacy was unable to persuade Najd to abandon its non-aligned position. Najd would fight neither the Turks in Iraq, as Britain wished, nor Sherif Hussein in Hejaz, as the Ottomans wished. With perspicacity, and given all the factors discussed above, Imam Abdul-Aziz saw the First World War merely as a colonial struggle by the great powers for control of the area.[57]

Britain tried repeatedly to win over the Imam, as shown by the actions of Captain Shakespear, who accompanied the Imam at the battle of Jarab, and Sir Percy Cox, who tried to entice Imam Abdul-Aziz by promises of a British endorsement of the transfer of the Caliphate to him. The Imam did not seem interested, which took Cox by surprise; he immediately cabled the information to London, so that it could be borne in mind when Sherif Hussein was contacted. But at the Darin, al-Qatīf and al-'Uqair meetings, the Imam had already warned Cox of the consequences of the Sherif of Mecca's speaking on behalf of the Arabs or appointing himself King of the Arabs. As a result, Britain recognized Hussein only as King of Hejaz.[58]

In 1917 a conference was held in Kuwait, convened by Sir Percy Cox, the British Civil Commissioner in Iraq; Sheikh Jabir al-Thani, son of Mubarak al-Sabah, the ruler of Kuwait; and Sheikh Khaz'al. Imam Abdul-Aziz was invited with the aim of investigating the situation, particularly when the so-called Arab revolt was seen to be imminent.[59]

In the same year, a delegation arrived from Bahrain to discuss with Imam Abdul-Aziz the possibility of a reconciliation with Sherif Hussein.[60] The delegation consisted of Hamilton, the British Political Officer and Consul; St John Philby; and Colonel Aden, the British Political Agent in Kuwait.

As previously mentioned, the area of Turba and al-Kharma was a bone of contention between Najd and Hejaz. Khalid bin Lu'ai, the Emir of al-Kharma, had been sent by Sherif Hussein to assist his son Abdullah in his siege of the Turkish garrison in al-Madīnah. Ibn Lu'ai, however, decided to desert Abdullah and return to al-Kharma, where he garrisoned his troops. When the Turkish garrison in al-Madīnah surrendered, Abdullah did not return to Mecca but instead headed for al-Kharma and Turba, seeking to occupy both, and succeeded in occupying the latter.

Imam Abdul-Aziz ordered Sultan Ibn Bijad, the most senior member of the *hijr* of al-Ghatghat, to go to al-Kharma and observe Abdullah's movements. When Turba was occupied, its people sought the help of Ibn Bijad. A famous battle took place, at which the Hashemite army was annihilated. The British Prime Minister speedily called the Cabinet to an extraordinary meeting, and the British government cabled Imam Abdul-Aziz through its Political Agent in Jiddah, requesting him not to advance to Taif. Imam Abdul-Aziz then received a letter from Reader Bullard, the British Consul in Jiddah, asking him to return to Najd in June 1919.[61]

In our discussion of the 'Uqair agreement, it will not have escaped the reader's attention that nothing was mentioned by either party about their commitments concerning the western border, i.e. that which separated Najd and Hejaz. Imam Abdul-Aziz then considered whether future relations between Najd and Hejaz could be settled between the two parties alone, or whether they were linked to British interests.[62] Until then, he did not know the extent to which Sherif Hussein was linked to Britain, or the extent of the promises made to him. But, when Sherif Hussein and his sons held a meeting in Mecca which was attended by a number of *ulema* and some figures from the Arab nationalist movement, and at which Hussein was proclaimed King of the Arabs, Imam Abdul-Aziz protested. However, as has been made clear, Britain reassured the Imam that, together with France, it recognized Hussein only as King of Hejaz.

Sir Reginald Wingate, the British High Commissioner in Egypt, had already written to Hussein as follows:

> I find it difficult to believe the news which I received that Your Majesty wished to sever the friendly relations with Ibn Saud. I request you most earnestly to do your utmost to prevent all motives leading to a misunderstanding regarding your policy towards the aforementioned Emir. We simply cannot ignore the fact that he is both influential and significant in Arab politics.[63]

Britain seemed to be of the opinion that the defeat of the Ottoman Empire in the First World War and its withdrawal from the Arab world had created a power vacuum which could only be filled by Imam Abdul-Aziz bin Saud.

The end of the world war was followed by the convening of the peace conference, the above-mentioned talks and contacts which ended with Iraq and Transjordan being placed under British mandates, and the establishment of the Kingdom of Iraq with Feisal bin Hussein as King, in addition to the rule of Sherif Hussein in Hejaz. The rulers of these states (which were under British mandate or ruled in alliance with Britain) were all from the same family. All these developments seemed to have tightened the noose around the Sultanate of Najd and its Dependencies.

In Kuwait, Sheikh Mubarak al-Sabah died in 1916; he was succeeded by his son Jabir, who died the following year. Jabir's brother, Sheikh Salim al-Mubarak al-Sabah, took over and relations between Najd and Kuwait deteriorated significantly. Imam Abdul-Aziz had authorized one of the chiefs of the Mutair to build a *hijr* round the waters of a village claimed by Sheikh Salim for Kuwait. Feisal al-Dawish responded by launching an attack on Kuwait. Salim sought the help of the British, who used their naval vessels and planes to frighten off al-Dawish and his force.

After the death of Sheikh Salim, his nephew Ahmad al-Jabir al-Sabah succeeded him in 1921. He visited Riyadh and entered into negotiations with Imam Abdul-Aziz. But Ahmad was not alone: he was accompanied by a British representative, Bird, who was there on behalf of the British government. Agreement was reached over the borders and a neutral zone was established. An agreement was concluded between Najd and Kuwait on 2 December 1922.[64] This paved the way for Britain's insistence on the convening of the Kuwait Conference, to which we shall return in more detail in Chapter 4.[65]

Imam Abdul-Aziz responded bravely to the way he was encircled by Britain, launching a series of attacks which resulted in the annexation of 'Asīr and its capital Abha, Hā'il and then the administrative district of al-Jof and Wādī al-Sarhan. Finally, there was the Buraida raid which took place in the heart of Transjordanian territory in the summer of 1923.[66] The Imam thus managed to keep the fighting away from the Sultanate of Najd.

Although Britain was realizing the dream it had entertained for more than a century, the country had a heavy burden of debt after the First World War. Establishing security and stability in the areas which Britain occupied also proved demanding, in terms both of troop deployment and cost, necessitating continued general conscription at a time when British soldiers, worn out by the war, were demanding demobilization and the taxpayers were urging lower taxes.[67]

Britain therefore started to concentrate its efforts on co-operation, the conclusion of agreements and the convening of conferences to settle some of the problems which had arisen before the war and been exacerbated by it. Sir Percy Cox was the British envoy in Tehran at the time. He was suddenly recalled to London and was appointed High Commissioner in Iraq to implement British policy in the area.[68]

The prevailing feeling in Iraq was that neither the Iraqi nor the British government had been able to prevent the attacks launched by the Najdi tribes. The *ulema* in Najaf convened a meeting in Karbala' in 1922 to which King Feisal of Iraq was invited. The British High Commissioner, however, warned the King that the meeting could prove an embarrassment to him if he demanded the immediate independence of Iraq. Negotiations concerning the conclusion of an agreement between Iraq and Britain were under way. The Karbala' Conference played a major role in mobilizing the press to arouse the Arab masses against the mandate and fuel criticism of the Iraqi–British agreement. In the same year, the Iraqi National Party was established; in response, the British High Commissioner adopted harsh measures to stamp out opposition to the mandate and the agreement.

It was then that Britain apparently became aware that the outstanding border problems would remain a constant source of trouble in Iraq.[69] Britain's need (explained above) to use the demarcation of borders as a prelude to Iraq's joining the League of Nations is a further reason why Britain was so keen to make the Kuwait Conference a success.

As far as Hejaz was concerned, Britain was intent on settling the question

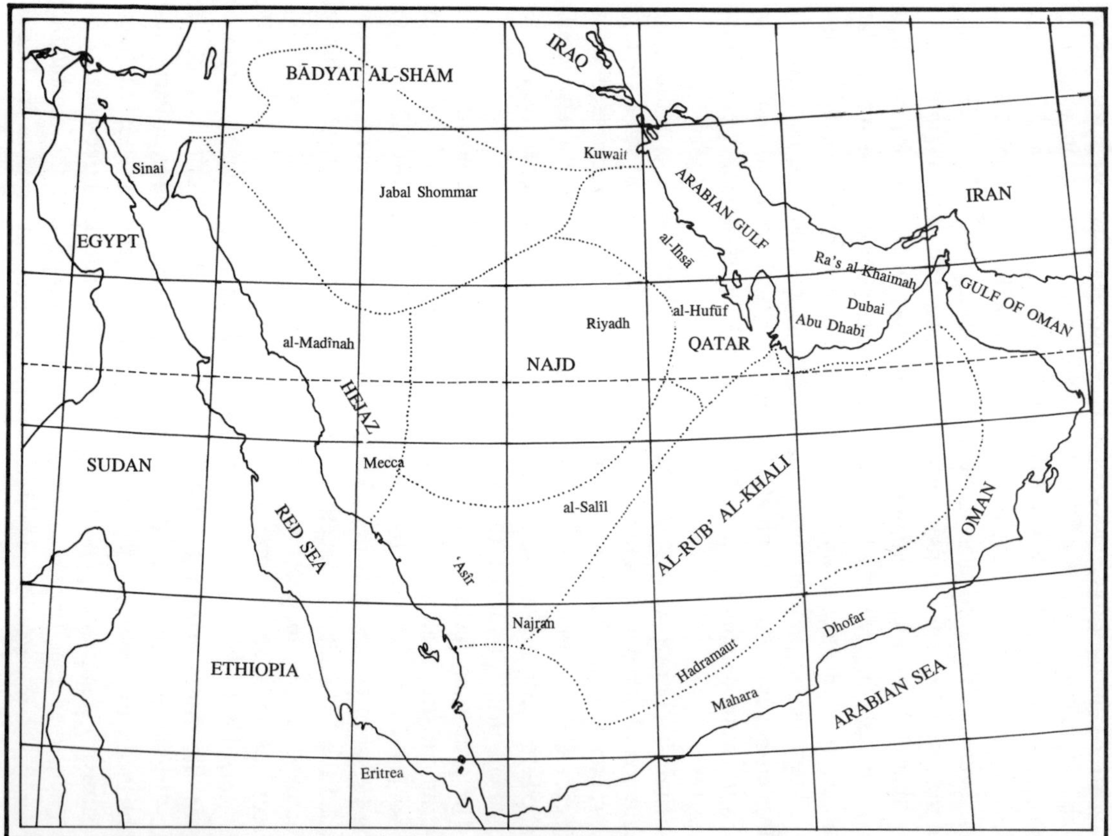

Map VI. The Sultanate of Najd and its Dependencies

of its relations with King Hussein, in order to arrive at an agreement on the basis of the Sykes–Picot agreement, as well as that of San Remo, and on the basis of the mandate. But Hussein was bent on opposing the mandate with one aim in mind, that of establishing a single Arab Kingdom, a demand which had been overtaken by recent events and circumstances, as explained above.[70]

Britain established a belt north and west of the Sultanate of Najd and its Dependencies as a means of unifying its policy and strategy. However, there were signs that this very aim of achieving political and strategic unity could be directed against Britain, building on the ambitions and intransigence of Sherif Hussein—particularly since the Sultanate of Najd and its Dependencies had now become the only power in the region capable of providing security and stability. Although the Muhammara treaty had been concluded between Najd and Iraq, and the two protocols of al-'Uqair had been signed, the border areas between the Sultanate of Najd and its Dependencies, on the one hand, and Iraq, Transjordan and Hejaz, on the other, were as uncertain as ever. This led Cox to call the Kuwait Conference in 1923–24.

4
The Kuwait Conference 1923–24

The Prelude to the Conference

In the previous chapter, we discussed how the border problems emerged and grew as the Sultanate of Najd and its Dependencies expanded. We also discussed the establishment of the Kingdom of Iraq and the Emirate of Transjordan, with King Hussein in Hejaz, and how these developments multiplied and complicated the problems referred to earlier.[1] In this connection, we referred to the Muhammara[2] agreement (1922), concluded between Iraq and the Sultanate of Najd, with the participation of Britain, an ally of Hejaz and the state under whose mandate both Iraq and Transjordan were placed.

As we pointed out, when the need to draw fixed borders for Iraq and to calm the situation there became urgent, the 'Uqair Conference was held in the same year, with Najd maintaining that the Dhufair clan, then settled in al-Shāmiyya in Iraq, were citizens of Najd, and that al-'Amarat and al-Rola were branches of the 'Anza, whose chief tribes, Banu al-Hathal and Banu Sha'lan, were also citizens of Najd. As the Sultan of Najd was able to regain what had been under the control of the Rashīd family, he would also be entitled to regain those who had slipped away or escaped from those areas.[3]

What was most significantly agreed, then, was the establishment of a neutral zone between Najd and Iraq to prevent inter-tribal clashes. It was stipulated that this zone would remain ungarrisoned and that the tribes living on the borders between the two countries would have access to grazing land and water in that area.[4]

The 'Uqair meeting resulted in the acceptance of the principle of border demarcation between Arab states, the determination of the borders between Najd and Iraq, the establishment of a neutral zone, the confirmation that al-Milh and Wādī al-Sarhan were both in Najd and the determination of which tribes belonged to which side. However, Iraq did not honour the agreement at the time, flouting particularly those clauses relating to the ban on building and the establishment of checkpoints in the border area. The border problems were also to grow in magnitude and become intractably complex as a result of the expansion of Najd's northern and north-eastern borders, especially after regaining al-Jof, Wādī al-Sarhan and the two oases of Taima' and Khaibar.[5]

The Sultanate of Najd demanded that the agreement be implemented, particularly with regard to the resettlement in Najd of the tribes of Shammar returning from Iraq. But Iraq kept stalling, while attacks and counter-attacks constantly erupted between the two sides. The situation became even more complicated when the Transjordan tribes plundered and killed men from the Najdi tribes passing through from Transjordan to Syria.[6]

Furthermore, as though unaware of the historic developments of the age, King Hussein began to demand that al-Jof and Wādī al-Sarhan be given to Transjordan and that Taima', Khaibar, Turba and al-Kharma be returned to him. He even demanded that Hā'il be returned to the Rashīd family, and 'Asīr to the 'Ayid family.

At that time, it seemed as though the problems between Najd, on the one hand, and Iraq, Transjordan and Hejaz, on the other, were so interconnected that one burning issue inevitably led to another.[7] The issue of the clans thus became the most significant problem in the eyes of the Najdi government. Raids continued between the tribes of northern Najd and those of the Iraqi desert. The early years of King Feisal's reign in Iraq saw no change in the situation, despite the 'Uqair Conference and the demarcation of the Najdi–Iraqi border.[8]

When the Iraqi Cabinet, at its session of 13 October 1922, agreed to publish the Iraqi–British treaty, it had already been decided that Winston Churchill, Secretary of State for the Colonies, would issue a communiqué in London on the same day. The communiqué stated that Britain would do its utmost to expedite the determination of the Iraqi borders so that Iraq could submit an application for membership of the League of Nations once the treaty and the other agreements provided for had been ratified. The communiqué also announced that Britain would do all in its power to persuade the League of Nations to accept Iraq as a member.[9]

It is worth noting that the meetings and conferences held in this period were dominated by economic issues on a par with the political issues. British companies were focusing on the prospect of discovering oil deposits and obtaining concessionary rights in Arab countries. Some of these companies even enjoyed the backing of Sir Percy Cox.

Shortly after the ‘Uqair Conference, Emir Abdullah bin Hussein dispatched an armed force in an attempt to occupy al-Milh.[10] Najd stepped in to deter such attempts, and Abdullah had to turn to the British government, which at the time felt that the matter could be settled by peaceful means.

In agreeing to the proclamation of Abdullah as Emir of Transjordan, Churchill had also agreed to the separation of al-Jof and its annexation to the Transjordan Emirate. Furthermore, the British were keen to let bygones be bygones as far as the causes of the conflict were concerned and hoped to work towards stabilizing the situation in this Arab region. Britain also wished to stop the aid which it was giving to some Arab countries, as part of curbing expenditure at the end of the First World War. It thus announced that all existing aid would be stopped from 31 March 1924, with the Exchequer handing out aid as a final settlement until that date.

Subsequently Britain felt that the solution to these problems would be for the Arab leaders to gather at a conference to be held in Kuwait towards the end of 1923 presided over by Britain. The aim of the conference would be to enable the leaders to discuss the causes and manifestations of the conflict and to reach an agreement regarding them.[11]

Britain chose Colonel Knox to chair the conference. Knox was about to retire from his post as first British Judicial Officer. Before occupying this position, he had been British Agent in Kuwait since 1903. Knox wanted to be personally involved in the settlement of these problems and thus succeed where so many of his predecessors, both officers and politicians like Cox and others, had failed. Knox was also determined that this should be done quickly, as he was nearing retirement and his official days were therefore numbered,[12] so he started issuing invitations immediately.

Before going into the details of the Kuwait Conference proceedings, it is perhaps instructive to refer to a report written by Kamil Efendi Fahmi, an Egyptian who accompanied Mrs Hogarth[13] on a trip to ‘Asīr and Tihama in the spring of 1922. Fahmi relates that he enjoyed a close relationship with a number of dignitaries and other high-ranking men there. He had spent some time with al-Sayyid Muhammad Ali al-Idrisi and, on his return from this trip, he found it useful to submit a report explaining the political position from his observations and contacts. Fahmi sent the report to Sir Gilbert Clayton, the former adviser to the Egyptian Ministry of the Interior, who had originally encouraged him to write such a report.

Fahmi stated how extremely surprised he was at the significant change of opinion among the people of these areas in the past year. While they used to view the British government in a spirit of trust and friendship, the attitude was now completely the opposite. There were two reasons for this, Fahmi explained: first, the help that Britain gave to the Greeks against the Ottoman Empire, which was essentially aimed at weakening Islam; and, second, Britain's support of the Sherif of Mecca, its attempt to proclaim him the Muslim Caliph, its naming him King of the Arabs and its attempt to subject the rest of the Emirs in the peninsula to his rule. This, the people of the area felt, was contrary to the real British view of the Sherif as merely a puppet. The report also referred to France's role in perpetuating this situation.[14]

The report then mentioned Mahmoud Pasha Nadim, a Turkish official and former *wāli* in Yemen. He lived in San'ā' and was an ardent supporter of the Turkish Kemalists and France. Nadim therefore kept in close contact with both parties, and the report confirmed that he was an important factor in the dissemination of their ideas in the area.

Fahmi went on to say that he had learned of the arrival of a number of French and Turkish officials in Djibouti, and then in Mecca. They were in close contact with Mahmoud Pasha Nadim. In San'ā' they were joined by Aziz Bey, a doctor, and Sayyid Bey Abdul-Samad, who then left for Istanbul, carrying messages from the delegates to Mustafa Kemal.

The report then touched on the envisaged Union of Arab States. Through discussions on this subject with Emir al-Idrisi, Fahmi learned that al-Idrisi was a faithful and sincere ally of Ibn Saud, who was then supplying him with all kinds of assistance. The two men also had a common bond in their hatred and rejection of the Sherif of Mecca. Any move by the Sherif would be met with decisive joint action by both these men. Fahmi advised them not to harm any of the existing regimes in the Arabian peninsula, but just to appease the Sherif of Mecca; otherwise, there would be turmoil throughout the peninsula.[15]

The report was a highly significant document. It shed light on the conditions which Britain saw as making the convening of the Kuwait Conference inevitable, and which in turn shaped Britain's position *vis-à-vis* the Sherif of Mecca. Britain thus convened the conference. Meanwhile Knox wrote to the Sultan of Najd:

> With reference to your correspondence concerning Qaf [one of the Aba al-Milh villages] which I received through our representative in Bahrain, I should like to relay to Your Majesty (in compliance with your command) that the British government is pleased with your ordering your

forces to cease fire. The government has also instructed me to present to Your Majesty its intention to convene a conference in Bahrain or in Kuwait as soon as possible to discuss the question of the Najd–Transjordan border. I am also instructed to put it to Your Majesty that it is possible to use this opportunity to discuss outstanding issues between Najd and Iraq, including the Shammar refugees. Finally, I am instructed to suggest to Your Majesty the possibility, if you so desire, of settling the problems between you and Hejaz; the British government is prepared to suggest the same to King Hussein.

The aim of the British government in this meeting is to clear up misunderstandings and solve all outstanding problems between the various neighbouring states.

As for the issue of Qaf, whether you or Transjordan have the upper hand, this will have no effect on the meeting and on the discussion of the aforementioned issues which will take place shortly.[16]

In September 1924 Imam Sultan Abdul-Aziz responded in the following terms:

Greetings,

I have received your letter, with the enclosed telegram, concerning the settlement of the problems between my government and the governments of Iraq, Transjordan and Hejaz, and the suggestion of the British government that a conference be convened in Bahrain or Kuwait, with the aim of determining the borders between Najd, Hejaz and Transjordan, and discussing the question of the Shammar tribe who sought refuge in Iraq.

I should like to determine the borders between my Kingdom and the governments of Hejaz and Transjordan, so that differences due to misunderstandings may be settled. Nothing would give me more pleasure than to be in agreement and on friendly terms with my neighbours. I have therefore agreed, with the utmost pleasure, to take part in this conference to be held either in Bahrain or in Kuwait.

However, I will not agree to the Iraqi delegate, together with the governments of Hejaz and Transjordan, taking part in the discussions; nor will I agree to the delegate of Transjordan together with Iraq, nor to the delegate of Hejaz together with any of these governments, taking part in such discussions.[17]

Imam Abdul-Aziz's reply clearly shows his great concern that the neighbouring states should not form blocs directed against the Sultanate of

Najd and its Dependencies.

On 1 November 1923 the British Representative in Jiddah received a telegram from the Foreign Office informing him that a conference would be convened in Kuwait on 15 November 1923 under the chairmanship of Colonel Knox, who was then the British Political Resident in the Gulf. The conference was to be attended by Najd, Iraq, Transjordan and Hejaz.

In examining the relevant documents, one may safely conclude that Britain fixed the date for the conference only after it had received Imam Abdul-Aziz's agreement in principle. The document, which included the telegram referred to above, mentioned that Ibn Saud had agreed to attend the conference, and that Abdullah and his brother Feisal were about to agree. The document also mentioned that the Sheikh of al-Muhammara would host the conference, and that King Hussein had sent notification that he would be sending a deputy with the necessary full powers to discuss the border problems between Najd and Hejaz. As soon as his mind was made up, King Hussein would cable Jerusalem to fly his representative from Amman in order to reach the conference in time.[18]

Imam Sultan Abdul-Aziz replied to the British Representative in Jiddah in the following terms:

> I have received your letter dated 2 November 1923. But we were taken by surprise over the decision to convene the conference on the date mentioned, which does not give us enough time even to choose a suitable representative, let alone being able to have such a representative arrive in time. To be able to respond positively to your request, I therefore find it necessary to ask you to appoint and dispatch to me someone from His Majesty's government well versed in Britain's policies in both the east and the west, to deliberate with me in advance of the conference. This I find absolutely essential.[19]

In a telegram to the Sultan of Najd, Knox expressed his utmost pleasure at the Sultan's decision to take part in the conference to discuss the following points: the Najd–Transjordan borders; the Najd–Hejaz borders; and a solution to the problem of the Shammar who sought refuge in Iraq. Knox added:

> I shall myself go to Bombay to fetch the clerks and items necessary for the conference. I estimate that I shall, God willing, be back in Kuwait on 14 November. I hope that this will give you enough time to choose deputies and grant them the necessary plenipotentiary powers. My government has instructed me to accept your conditions that the

representatives of each country shall only speak for the matters which concern their own country.[20]

On 27 November 1923 Imam Sultan Abdul-Aziz sent Knox, chairman designate of the Kuwait Conference, a letter informing him that, with reference to the correspondence regarding the conference, the Sultan of Najd and its Dependencies had appointed Hamza Ghawth, Abdullah al-Damluji, Hafiz Wahba, Abdul-Aziz bin Hasan al-Qusaibi and Hashim bin Ahmad al-Rifa'i to conduct discussions with the deputies of the other governments; Ghawth would be chairman of the delegation, and al-Rifa'i secretary. Finally, the Sultan wished the conference all success.[21]

It is important to note here that at the time there were no differences between the Sultanate of Najd and Iraq over the issue of the borders and the tribes, as these had been settled in the Muhammara treaty of May 1922 and its annexes signed at al-'Uqair. The only differences were over the return of the Shammar tribes who had sought refuge in Iraq and the loot they had brought with them.

King Hussein was informed of the conference and the date on 15 November 1923 in a letter from the British deputy Consul requesting him to send representatives to Amman in order to fly to Kuwait as soon as possible.[22] The King replied in a letter addressed to the British Agent in Jiddah dated 3 November 1923, stating that he had received the letter of invitation dated 2 November 1923 with the utmost respect and appreciation, and that he was particularly grateful for Britain's sympathies with the Arabs as shown by its calling a conference to be held in Kuwait. However, the King expressed his surprise at the decision to go ahead and at the date fixed, which did not give him sufficient time to think of a suitable representative, even if such a representative were able to arrive in time for the conference.[23]

In response, the British Representative in Jiddah contacted the Foreign Office in telegram no. 52, dated 4 November 1923, informing them that the King thanked the British government but refused the invitation to the Kuwait Conference on the grounds that he had been given very little time and had not been properly consulted in advance.[24]

The British Foreign Office replied to the British Representative in Jiddah in a telegram dated 6 November 1923, instructing him to explain to the King that the conference had originally been planned to settle the problems of Iraq and Transjordan, and that was why he had not been consulted in advance. Faced with the intransigence of King Hussein, the Foreign Office in its telegram deemed it appropriate to postpone the conference for a week, that is, until 22 November, and instructed the British Representative in Jiddah to urge the King to take part. The Representative was also instructed to explain that a solution to the problems between Najd and Hejaz was in the interests of Hejaz, and that the British government saw this as a valuable opportunity which should not be lost.[25]

With this in mind, the British Representative sent King Hussein a letter dated 7 November 1923, relaying as speedily as possible the view of the British government, namely, that the Kuwait Conference was originally conceived to discuss the urgent problems of Iraq and Transjordan, which affected Britain directly; that the Hejaz–Najd border problem essentially differed from the Iraq–Transjordan border problem, a difference which explained why the British government had not consulted the King in advance; and, finally, that the British government saw the discussion at such a conference of the Hejaz problems, together with many other problems, preferable to discussing them individually in another forum.[26]

But in a letter two days later, King Hussein replied to the British representative that, while he was appreciative of Britain's advice and its observations concerning Arab affairs, he was nevertheless unable to reconcile such an attitude and the decision to convene the Kuwait Conference, on the one hand, and, on the other, the letter which he had received from the British High Commissioner in Egypt dated 30 August 1915 as well as the correspondence he had had with the British during the war. The King then requested that an expert from the British government be sent to discuss the matter with him and reach some understanding, noting that all he was asking for was a little more time for reflection and consultation.

The King went on to say:

> The fact that I have thrown all my weight behind this, with all the known risks and possible ruin, only goes to prove that my intentions are clear and above board. But I was informed only after everything had been settled, and a conference decided on to deal with the affairs of us all in the Arabian peninsula. A statement explicitly speaking on behalf of all concerned was also included in the letter of the High Commissioner of Egypt dated 30 August 1915, and in all the other government correspondence during the war and right up to the armistice. I would not hesitate to say that, with the providence of Allah, we have up to the present moment loyally and resolutely done our utmost to live up to Great Britain's expectations of me and my people. This is proven by the fact that we have rejected a unilateral reconciliation, which the letter of His Majesty's Foreign Ministry dated 8 February 1918 confirms.
>
> My request that one of Great Britain's expert advisers be sent for discussion and consultation with me on this subject is further proof of the sincerity of my intentions and my concern to fulfil my commitments and

show my gratitude for the good done us by the British. You are no doubt aware of this, as you show in the first part of your letter when speaking of matters that have a direct impact on His Majesty's government. As I pointed out to you in my letter of August 1918, there is something behind all this unrest, intrigue and rebellion that would not be in my own interest, or be of any benefit to me personally or give His Majesty's government cause to doubt the sincerity of my intentions.

The present situation in the entire country from north to south and from east to west gives cause for alarm. To prevent any deterioration of this situation, I have requested discussion and consultation with an official from Great Britain. My sole motive in this is my concern to safeguard our mutual interest and it is natural to seek that which has already yielded positive results. From my point of view, the least that could now come out of this is that I have acted responsibly and in a manner which my own conscience dictated and which only heeds what is of mutual interest to both of us.

The parties involved in the conference will be totally powerless. This is demonstrated by the lack of any prior understanding. I do not know if the sorrow and despair which I at present feel for refusing your request to take part in this conference would be greater than that which I will feel for accepting the annexation of Hejaz. The latter alternative seems to be the upshot of Your Excellency's speaking of 'seizing the opportunity to discuss outstanding matters between Hejaz and Najd'.

Your Excellency, Hejaz is a part of the peninsula of our ancestors which Great Britain has specially chosen for the Arabs to regain their past glory and for our mutual interests to be safeguarded. The only concern which Hejaz has is therefore to protect itself from any infringement of this status. We will have no difficulty in ascribing any infringement of this as an infringement of the honour of Britain and nothing could be greater or more serious than what amounts to such an infringement in the reference you make in the first part of your letter. Indeed, the effect would be precisely such an infringement.

Faced with the seriousness of the situation and the need to shed light on the issues involved, the least I can do is to remind His Majesty's government of the statement made by its Foreign Secretary in his letter dated 8 February 1918 mentioned above, saying that His Majesty's government is insistent on ridding the Arabs of the injustices that have befallen them. Is not the British government's attitude to go along with the annexation of the Emirate of 'Asīr, al-'Ayid and al-Rashīd or any other area to the Sultanate of Najd tantamount to twice the injustice already committed by forcing the Wahabi doctrine on these people and

> the elimination of their own religious beliefs? Such violations run counter to statements made by Great Britain that it is intent on standing behind the Arab nation in its struggle to rebuild an Arab world in which, instead of Ottoman injustice, only law and order would prevail.
>
> These statements continued to the point where they reiterated the pledge previously made by His Majesty the King of Britain to support the liberation of the Arabian lands, to protect those liberated Arabs from falling into the abyss of destruction and to assist those still under the yoke of tyranny in regaining their freedom.
>
> There was another pledge. This relates to opposing the change of doctrine by force and the imposition of the death sentence on those who refuse to surrender even if what is being rejected happens to be European standards of law and order. Those who had been trodden upon by the Wahabi doctrine could therefore only look to Britain, appealing to its honour and fair-mindedness and invoking its concern that its explicit promises and undertakings relayed through its Foreign Ministry mentioned above would be fulfilled. I implore Great Britain not to take the points I have just raised as emanating from protest but as an appeal to its conscience and noble sentiments.[27]

In the light of Britain's desire to settle all outstanding problems in the Arabian peninsula—particularly between the Sultanate of Najd and its Dependencies, on the one hand, and its neighbours to the north and the west, on the other—King Hussein's letter and the issues raised were sufficient to make Britain reluctant to give him assistance. Hence the comment of the British Representative, who sent the King's letter with an enclosed translation to the Foreign Office in London, saying that the King had not responded to the deadline for taking part in the conference, and instead had sent a lengthy letter saying that Britain should not call any conference for the settlement of any problem relating to the Arabs without prior consultation with him.[28]

The British Foreign Office sent the British Representative in Jiddah a copy of the instructions relayed to Bushire (in Iran), Baghdad, Jerusalem and Colonel Knox, containing an overall picture of the envisaged outcome of the Kuwait Conference. The gist of this was that Emir Abdullah would relinquish Qaf in return for acquiring Aqaba, that Ibn Saud would withdraw from al-Kharma and Turba in return for Qaf, and that King Hussein would give up all his claims in the area north of al-Mudawwara. The Foreign Office instructions to Colonel Knox also recommended that, in the case of King Hussein's insistence that he would not attend the conference, Knox should secure a written undertaking from Ibn Saud that he would withdraw from Turba and al-Kharma in return for Qaf.[29]

On the same date, the Foreign Office sent another telegram to Bushire, Baghdad, Jerusalem and Colonel Knox, expressing the utmost concern over the possibility of postponing the conference to the following year, and over Ibn Saud's saying that he might arrive in Kuwait in the first week of December. The telegram also pointed out that Britain might be obliged to use its navy to impose an economic embargo on the Sultanate of Najd and its Dependencies, and that Knox had been notified of this warning; hence his departure for Bombay on 16 November.[30]

For his part, King Feisal of Iraq agreed to attend the conference, announcing that he had appointed his Minister of Public Works, Sabih Bey Nash'at, as his representative, and had given him the necessary powers to discuss outstanding issues and to sign the appropriate documents. In his notification, King Feisal wished the conference success, and hoped that friendship and brotherhood would finally prevail in all parts of the Arabian peninsula.[31]

Meanwhile, the credentials of Ali Khulqi Bey, Minister of Education, had been forwarded to the British Representative in Kuwait, nominating him as the representative of Transjordan at the Kuwait Conference. The papers stated that, in accordance with advice from Britain that Transjordan should take part in the prospective conference in Kuwait in the first week of December 1923, Khulqi Bey had been appointed representative and had been given full powers to sign whatever measures the conference decided on.[32]

In the letter of appointment from Emir Abdullah of Transjordan to his representative, it was stated that Khulqi Bey had been sent to discuss the establishment of peace between the two Emirates of Iraq and Transjordan, on the one hand, and, on the other, Emir Abdul-Aziz bin Abdul-Rahman bin Feisal al-Saud, ruler of Riyadh, al-Hasa, al-Kharj, al-Qasīm and Wādī al-Dawasir, and head of the tribes of central and southern Najd. The letter also stated that the bearer had full powers to negotiate with the representative of Abdul-Aziz separately and, if necessary, jointly in the presence of the representative of the King of Iraq, within the instructions given to him. The representative of Emir Abdullah also had the authority to sign whatever measures the conference resolved upon within the instructions given to him.[33]

On 2 December 1923 the British Political Representative resident in Bushire cabled the British Representative that the Kuwait Conference might collapse if Ibn Saud felt that the Hashemites were all opposing him. The telegram also referred to Knox's arrival in Kuwait on 30 November 1923, and suggested that King Hussein could now be pressured into sending his representative by rail to Damascus and then on to Baghdad without delay.[34]

The Foreign Office then cabled the British Representative, asking if it was possible that King Hussein might still change his mind and soften his position. The Representative was asked to take any measures necesssary to help achieve this result.[35] But he replied that, as far as he could tell, any other invitation to King Hussein to take part in the Kuwait Conference would be met only by a flat refusal.[36]

On 8 December 1923 Knox cabled from Kuwait that the Saudi delegation headed by Hamza Ghawth had arrived in Bahrain on its way to the conference, and that the conference could therefore be held on 17 December 1923. In another telegram on the same day, Knox said that Iraq and Transjordan had declared that it was possible to sign an agreement with Najd, provided that Najd sign another satisfactory agreement with Hejaz. Given this, Knox continued, it was possible that further efforts could persuade King Hussein to take part in the conference.[37]

According to a telegram sent by Knox from Kuwait to the British Representative, the Najdi delegation arrived in Kuwait on 16 November 1923.[38] The following day, Knox received a telegram from the British Representative informing him that it was now certain that Hejaz would not be sending a representative to the conference.[39]

The Three Phases of the Conference

The conference convened its first session on 17 December 1923. The Iraqi delegation stated its demands as follows:

> An agreement shall be drawn up between Najd and Iraq which prevents tribal raids, and communications between His Majesty the Sultan of Najd and his tribes which settle in Iraq shall be conducted exclusively through his representative in Baghdad, while communications between the government of Iraq and its tribes settling in Najd shall be conducted exclusively through its representative to be appointed in Baghdad.
>
> His Majesty the Sultan of Najd may not communicate directly with Iraqi officials or tribal leaders. The government of Iraq undertakes to do the same concerning communications with Najd's officials and tribal leaders.
>
> The Sultan of Najd may ask for military detachments, composed of his own tribes settled in Iraq, and in the event that these detachments are needed by the Sultan, they are free to answer his call. Those who do, however, must leave Iraq with their families. The government of Iraq shall do the same with its tribes in Najd.

> Unless agreed by both parties, neither Iraqi nor Najdi troops shall cross the borders of either country with the aim of tracking down criminals.
>
> A separate agreement shall be concluded for the extradition of criminals, who are to be subsequently proven guilty of non-political crimes before courts recognized by both parties.
>
> Each party shall appoint an official to be called the Inspector of the Borders, who shall be accompanied by no more than twenty men all of whom shall reside in a specified area, for the purpose of checking on tribes crossing the borders and reporting to their respective governments. The two Inspectors shall also function as intermediaries through whom loot and stolen property are exchanged, and shall seek to prevent theft and transgressions. They may also be granted other powers.[40]

In the second session, held on 18 December 1923, the Najdi delegation presented its demands as follows:

> The Najdi Shammar tribes shall be returned to Najd.
>
> All the loot, as specified in the attached list, stolen from Najdi citizens after the 'Uqair agreement shall be returned.
>
> Criminals and brigands from Najdi tribes who seek refuge in Iraq shall be extradited.
>
> If it is felt that the settlement of a particular tribe would disturb public security and cause unrest through trouble-making and transgressions, the government of either party shall be entitled to expel those involved. In such cases, the government on whose territory such people reside must comply with requests from the other government.[41]

Knox cabled the proceedings of this session to the Colonial Office in London, with copies to Baghdad, Jerusalem and Bushire. He relayed the Iraqi view that the Shammar tribes had settled on the Turkish border and that any attempt directed against them would only result in the infiltration of that border, contravening international law.[42] Knox also mentioned that he had received word from Bullard in Jiddah to the effect that there was no hope of Hejaz's sending a delegation to the conference, a development which had strengthened the hand of the Najdi delegation.

Knox also pointed out that another issue had been raised in this session. This related to whether it was possible to declare that a raid was a crime punishable by expulsion and legal proceedings, and whether those seeking refuge were liable to be handed back to their governments. The Najdi delegation stated that it was prepared to sign an extradition agreement for the exchange of criminals. The Iraqi delegate, however, responded that this was impossible.[43]

As for the question of loot, the Iraqi government was of the opinion that nothing seized prior to the formation of the Iraqi government was to be returned. The Najdi delegation, however, felt that, in accordance with international law, the date of the Muhammara and 'Uqair agreements was an appropriate cut-off point.[44]

As far as the Iraqi demands were concerned, the Najdi delegation maintained the following points:

> Najd agrees to conclude an agreement for the prevention of tribal raids.
>
> Communication between governments shall be conducted through the Inspector of the Borders.
>
> Najd wholeheartedly accepts than an agreement be concluded for the extradition of prisoners, on condition that inter-tribal raids are considered in principle crimes whose perpetrators must be handed over to their governments. Political crimes must be distinguished from other crimes. A commission agreed by both parties shall regulate other related matters.

Knox noted the intransigence of Sabih Bey Nash'at and wrote to Sir Henry Dobbs, the British High Commissioner in Baghdad, informing him of this observation. Knox noted that, although all he had to say could be summarized in five minutes, Sabih Bey was talkative, constantly trying to score points against the Najdi delegation and hardly giving them the opportunity to speak.

Knox pointed out that if the aim was to promote goodwill between his government and that of Ibn Saud, a more conducive atmosphere must be created in which the Najdi delegation felt that its views were worthy of consideration. It was vital, therefore, that the Najdi delegation be heard with magnanimity and patience. Knox went on to say that Sabih Bey had made such a negative impression on the other delegates that everybody felt he ought to take the first boat out of Kuwait.

Knox explained that Ibn Saud demanded the return of the Shammar tribes and all those who had escaped from his kingdom. He also demanded that in future all those seeking refuge in Iraq must be returned. The Najdi delegation was right to argue that without the implementation of these measures there would be no peace on the border. But all Sabih Bey had to say to these demands was 'No! Impossible!', a most obstructionist attitude to take. In conclusion, Knox wondered if it was possible for Dobbs to send Sabih Bey some advice.[45]

At the fifth session of the conference, the chairman proposed that the article concerning raids be rephrased as follows:

(a) Each of the two contracting parties shall recognize that raids by its own tribes who are settled on territory which borders that of the other state are crimes whose perpetrators must be severely punished, and that the head of the tribe committing such a crime shall be held personally responsible.

(b) In addition to what is stated in paragraph (a), the two states are answerable as far as possible, once a claimant has sufficient proof of looting and of the size of the loot, for the return of the goods looted or, failing that, the payment of compensation.

(c) To prove that looting has occurred and to determine the size of the loot, a commission shall be established which comprises representatives from the two states. It shall meet in the place of the party against whom a claim has been made, shall have the right to hear testimony and seek evidence from both parties, and shall pass judgments that are binding on both parties.

(d) Should differences between the two parties arise over whether the crime of looting has been committed and the amount looted, and where the above-mentioned commission is unable to settle them, the matter shall be referred to an arbitration commission comprising the British High Commissioner in Iraq and the official in charge of the Gulf region. The judgment of the latter commissions shall be accepted as binding on the two parties.

Here, the two parties agreed that some of the delegates should meet to formulate the articles that had been agreed in principle so far.[46]

Knox's telegram to the Representative in Jiddah on 22 December 1923 underlined the difficulties encountered that morning in attempting to formulate the protocols that had been agreed between the two parties. The telegram also stated that these attempts had collapsed as a result of Iraq's demand that a condition be incorporated in the protocols, namely that this agreement should be deemed effective only after an agreement had been reached between Hejaz and Najd. The Najdi delegation immediately rejected this condition as it was tantamount to recognition of an undeclared union between Iraq and Hejaz, directed against Najd.

Knox also mentioned that, faced with this situation, he saw no use in continuing with the conference as long as Hejaz had not sent a delegation. This was a regrettable decision, of course. Furthermore, the delegations of Najd and Iraq requested that negotiations between them be adjourned until 18 January 1924, a period which would give the Iraqi representative the opportunity to consult with his government and consider matters over which there were differences before proceeding with the negotiations. The postponement would also give the Najdi delegation a similar opportunity to deliberate with the Sultan of Najd. Finally, Knox reaffirmed that these issues could not be settled without King Hussein's also sending a representative. Thus, Knox permitted the Iraqi delegation to make a quick visit to Baghdad, while negotiations proceeded between Najd and Transjordan.[47]

When reviewing the conference proceedings, the manoeuvrings, the topics under discussion, the points of agreement and the points of difference, together with the contacts undertaken to persuade King Hussein to take part in the conference, it is of vital importance to refer to a telegram from the British Foreign Office to Reader Bullard, dated 17 December 1923, in response to an earlier telegram (no. 59) which Bullard had sent. The Foreign Office telegram contained a directive from the Foreign Secretary endorsing Bullard's opinion that it was futile to make any further attempt to persuade King Hussein to take part in the Kuwait Conference.

The Foreign Office thus felt that if, at some future date, Ibn Saud were to launch an attack on Hejaz, it would be up to Bullard to handle any complaints and requests for assistance he might receive from King Hussein, bearing in mind the King's refusal to make use of the mediation efforts that were being exerted at the time of the Kuwait Conference by the British government.[48]

We may also refer to the telegram which the Foreign Office received from the British Representative on 25 December 1923, stating that King Hussein was on his way to Transjordan. The purpose of the trip was to destroy the Kuwait Conference, and to punish the British government for meddling in Arab affairs without consulting him.[49]

The delegation of Transjordan submitted its government's demands at the sixth session held on 23 December 1923 and at the seventh session held three days later. These included the following points:

> The government of Transjordan adheres to the main resolutions agreed by the British government and the government of His Majesty the King of Hejaz, namely that it would be incumbent on the government of His Majesty the King of Hejaz and his supporters to respect the contractual relations which existed at the time of the Ottoman Empire. The government of Transjordan therefore demands that the border between it and Najd be established on the basis of the above consideration.
>
> The government of Transjordan is prepared to accept that the border between it and Najd be worked out on the basis of former undertakings and borders, and in accordance with the agreement concluded by the

> Najdi government and the government of Great Britain on 18 July 1916, provided that the Najdi government relinquishes al-Jof and Sakaka and the area which belongs to them to Ibn Sha'lan so that this area becomes an inviolable Emirate in its own right. This Emirate is also vital for communications between Transjordan and Iraq in the future, and must therefore be left under the jurisdiction of the government of Transjordan.
>
> Plenipotentiary representatives may be appointed to reside in the capitals of the two countries and thus function as intermediaries between the two governments.
>
> The two governments of Transjordan and Najd must undertake to prevent raids on each other's territory. In the event of the occurrence of such incidents, the government whose tribes initiate a raid shall be bound to return the loot, or make restitution in kind, or pay money and the *diyyat* (blood money) for those killed if death is involved.[50]

Knox sent a telegram from Kuwait to the Secretary of State for the Colonies, informing him that the Jordanian delegation had submitted its demands and that counter-demands would be submitted by the Najdi delegation in the session scheduled for that day, 26 December 1923. More immediately, however, the Najdi delegation decided to refer to the Sultan the matter of the exchange of representatives. The Najdi delegation also protested against the claim of both Hejaz and Transjordan that they speak on behalf of all the Arabs, including those of al-Rola.[51]

Knox said that he believed the problem of al-Rola to be closely linked with the problem of the ownership of Wādī al-Sarhan. Transjordan claimed that it pertained to the Syrian tribes, was part of Syria and therefore belonged to Transjordan. The Najdi delegation, on the other hand, maintained that it had been under the control of Ibn Rashīd for 120 years.

In order to maintain a point of contact with Iraq, the Jordanian delegation sought to substantiate its claims regarding Wādī al-Sarhan. Najd, however, felt that the significance of Wādī al-Sarhan lay in giving its tribes the freedom to move away from the French in Syria.[52] At this session, the Najdi delegation responded as follows:

> The present government of Najd, which Sultan Abdul-Aziz has established on such solid foundations, is not something recent. For anyone who cares to look into the modern history of Najd, the roots of this government go back a long way.[53] If one were to go by theories put forward by the representative of Transjordan, one would be entitled to adduce numerous things. However, we are not aware of a single justification which entitled the King of Hejaz or the Emir or Transjordan

to speak the way they did or interfere as they were doing in the affairs of other Arab Emirates, particularly as these never had anything to bind them to Hejaz or Transjordan. Therefore, we refuse to look into the demand made by the representative of Transjordan in this respect.

Al-Jof, Sakaka and Wādī al-Sarhan in its entirety have always shared the same developments and vicissitudes as Najd. We therefore reject the demand made by the representative of Transjordan that Najd relinquish al-Jof and Sakaka.[54]

With the intention of removing the obstacles blocking the negotiations, the Najdi delegation demanded, first, that the representative of Transjordan speak on behalf of his government only and, second, that he precisely define the point of difference between Najd and Transjordan.

In the eighth session, held on the following day, the Najdi delegation made the following points:

Wādī al-Sarhan and al-Jof have been part of Najd since the first Saudi state.

Najd categorically rejects any point of contact between the government of Transjordan and the government of Iraq. Furthermore, the government of Najd must have borders which link up with those of Syria in order to secure its trade route.

The tribes in al-Jof and Wādī al-Sarhan belong to Najd.[55]

What made the Najdi delegation even more resistant to Transjordanian demands was that the chairman of the conference, Colonel Knox, tended to favour the Jordanians. In a telegram to the Secretary of State for the Colonies in London, dated 29 December 1923, Knox stated that he considered al-Nufud to be the northern border of the Sultanate of Najd and that Wādī al-Sarhan belonged to Syria. He also thought that Khaibar, Turba and al-Kharma should be given to Hejaz and that Najd should relinquish these areas, drawing its border to the east of those parts.[56]

The Jordanian delegation then responded to the demands of the Najdi delegation. The Jordanians insisted that al-Jof and Sakaka, together with the areas which belonged to them, were part of the Syrian territory whose borders started at Mada'in Salih and ended on the Euphrates. They also argued that the government of Transjordan was part of Syria, a claim which implied that al-Jof, Sakaka and Wādī al-Sarhan were grazing lands and an area for all the tribes which belonged to Transjordan.

The Jordanian delegate continued his response at the ninth session held on 2 January 1924, saying that unless the government of Najd relinquished al-Jof, Sakaka, Wādī al-Sarhan and all the territories of Hejaz which it had been claiming, with Turba, al-Kharma, Hā'it, Huwait, Wādī Bisha, Wādī Shahran, and parts of Banu Shahr, Bilhumur and Bilsumur country, and unless it drew the border between Hejaz and Najd with the desert being the decisive demarcation line, there would be no agreement.

At this point, Knox rose and said that neither the Iraqis nor the Jordanians had the right to talk about Hejaz, that Britain could not accept talk about Ibn Rashīd, and that when the Sultan of Najd had agreed to take part in the conference, he had laid down one basic condition, namely that no government be entitled to take part in discussions of the affairs of another country.[57] At this point, the first phase of the Kuwait Conference ended. Negotiations ceased and the representatives of both Transjordan and Iraq returned home.

In a telegram sent from Kuwait to the British Secretary of State for the Colonies, Knox said that the Jordanian representative to the Kuwait Conference had shown him a telegram from Emir Abdullah of Transjordan asking him to return to receive new instructions, and to report to the government on the conference proceedings. Knox added that on the following day, negotiations between Najd and Iraq would resume, as Sabih Bey Nash'at, the representative of Iraq, had returned the day before and that, as chairman of the conference, he (Knox) had allowed Ali Khulqi Bey to leave that day for Basra. Knox emphasized that Khulqi would exert every effort to make his trip as short as possible, promising to return by 1 February 1924. Knox reported that there were rumours that Ibn Saud had arrived at al-Hasa two days before. There was no confirmation from Bahrain, however, and the rumours were therefore not to be believed.[58]

On 3 January 1924 the British High Commissioner in Iraq cabled the Secretary of State for the Colonies with the outcome of his contacts with Sabih and Feisal: first, regarding the expulsion of those who sought refuge in Iraq, it was impossible generally to accept the principle of expulsion, as similar conditions existed on the borders between Iraq, Syria and Iran; and, second, regarding the issue of the raids, it was proposed that a special tribunal be set up with full powers to adjudicate on the matter. Feisal had also promised that the agreement with Najd would not be linked with that between Najd and Hejaz.[59]

The following day, the British High Commissioner in Iraq cabled the Secretary of State for the Colonies, informing him that Feisal saw no use in sending Sabih back before hearing Ibn Saud's view regarding what Feisal had said in the previous telegram. Feisal also needed Sabih in Iraq for the Turkish oil negotiations and the British treaty.[60]

Two days later, Knox cabled the Secretary of State that he felt it was premature to set up tribunals to look into inter-tribal transgressions.[61] Feisal also thought that at present it was not possible to hand the Shammar tribe over. However, he was prepared, formally and in writing, to undertake that the government of Iraq would expel those Shammaris who launched raids on Najd from Iraqi territory.[62]

The telegram sent from Kuwait to the Secretary of State showed how concerned Knox was about the delayed return of Sabih, which he saw as regrettable. Knox was worried that this delay might displease Abdul-Aziz bin Saud, and expressed the hope that the delay would be as short as possible and that the outstanding differences would be settled once and for all.

Knox also pointed out that it was possible to settle all the issues being discussed at the Kuwait Conference with the exception of placing an Iraqi representative in Najd, which would doubtless be unacceptable to Sultan Abdul-Aziz. Knox intimated that the immediate return of the Iraqi representative would please him greatly. It would also please him if the Sultan of Najd agreed to receive the representative of Iraq, an act which would in effect mean the existence of a direct link between Iraq and Najd.[63]

The Secretary of State for the Colonies instructed Knox to avoid encouraging the negotiators to adopt the notion that Britain should be an arbiter in the event of an agreement breaking down. Devonshire stated that it was enough that the chairman of the conference was Britain's Representative in Kuwait, and that any agreement reached should be signed by all parties, with the British government shouldering part of the responsibility in this respect.[64]

On 10 January 1924 the British High Commissioner in Iraq sent a report to the Secretary of State for the Colonies entitled *The Arab Borders*, with copies to the Air Ministry and the Government of India. The report referred to the return to Baghdad, on 30 December 1923, of Sabih Bey, the Iraqi representative to the Kuwait Conference, with the permission of Knox. Sabih Bey had gone to report to King Feisal on the conference proceedings and either he or a substitute would return as representative. The report then mentioned the demands of the Najdi delegation referred to above, concluding that King Feisal would issue a fresh set of instructions to this representatives on the following points:

> Regarding the expulsion of the tribes which sought refuge in Iraq, the government of Iraq cannot generally accept the principle of expulsion, so as not to cause disturbance on the borders with Syria, Turkey and Iran where conditions similar to those between Iraq and Najd exist.
>
> Regarding the prevention of raids, there is a proposal for the setting up of a special tribunal, comprising members from Iraq, Najd and a third

party to be chosen by the claimant, whose decision shall be adopted on a majority basis.

Regarding the Shammar of Najd, the Iraqi government undertakes to expel anyone engaging in attacks on Najdi tribes.

Regarding loot, the Iraqi government adheres to its originally stated position, namely that its responsibility dates from the day of King Feisal's coronation.

Iraq has retreated from its earlier preparedness to enter into an agreement regarding the extradition of non-political criminals.[65]

The report also mentioned that Sabih Bey had strongly condemned King Hussein's refusal to send a representative to the Kuwait Conference and that Sabih Bey was convinced that the King of Hejaz was not popular among the tribes and that his subjects would rather be under the Wahabi kingdom. The report pointed out that King Feisal himself was aware of his father's autocratic rule, unpopularity and opinionated behaviour. Sabih Bey went even further and spoke about the incompetence of the Transjordanian representative and the absurdity of his demands.[66]

Meanwhile, the British High Commissioner in Baghdad cabled the Secretary of State for the Colonies that the expansion of the Sultanate of Najd hampered a British project to lay railway track and pipelines from Iraq to Palestine. The High Commissioner stated that, in his opinion, the problem would be solved by keeping a wide strip of desert land under direct British control.[67] The previous day, Knox had warned the Secretary of State about Najd's insistence on its demands in the north, adding that what he saw as 'exaggerated' demands would render ineffective a border agreement between (French) Syria and Palestine and Transjordan.[68]

The Kuwait Conference began its second phase with a resumption of the negotiations between Najd and Iraq at the tenth session. Here, discussions continued on the basis laid down by King Feisal for his representative, referred to in the report of the British High Commissioner in Baghdad. In this and the following sessions, Knox said that he did not think it possible to consider raids a crime for which the culprits were to be sent back to their government, nor could the government of Iraq undertake to refuse those Najdis who sought refuge or hand them back to the Sultan of Najd. But Knox also noted that he did not see why Iraq should continue to reserve the right to accept any who sought refuge when such refugees abused their status and used the host country as a base for their aggression. He then suggested that the government of Iraq should not allow Najdi tribes to cross its borders without a guarantee, and that members of the Shammar tribe of Najd settled in Iraq should either give such guarantees or leave Iraq.[69]

Knox expressed his displeasure that the conference sessions were protracted and indecisive, and proposed that an interim settlement be signed for the items agreed so far. He also informed the conference that the British government would not want to be an arbiter of differences that might arise between two governments. However, his mediation efforts as chairman of the conference and as a British representative would always be at the disposal of all.[70] The Najdi representative replied that the most important issue for his government was that of the criminal tribes which sought refuge in Iraq. He refused to sign any agreement which did not settle these disputes and end these acts of aggression.

On the same day which saw the start of the second phase of the conference proceedings, the British Foreign Office informed the British Representative in Jiddah that Ibn Saud had written to the British Resident Representative in Bushire on 3 January 1924, expressing his surprise at rumours that King Hussein had finally refused to take part in the Kuwait Conference, that the King had mobilized an expeditionary force which had set out from al-Madīnāh and was then stationed in Harimla, that Ibn Saud had given strict instructions to his generals and troops not to attack the Hejaz border, and that if he did not receive a written undertaking from the British government that Hejazi troops would not attack Najd he would not be held responsible for the consequences. The Foreign Office asked the Resident Representative to look into these rumours.[71] Trevor in Bushire had relayed the same information to the British Representative in Jiddah a few days before.[72]

The British Representative in Jiddah replied to the Foreign Office that King Hussein's refusal to take part in the Kuwait Conference could be neither accepted nor justified. The Representative denied the rumour that Hussein was mobilizing troops on the Najdi border, pointing out that the pressure, rather than coming from the King's side, was in fact coming from Ibn Saud.[73]

At this point, the British High Commissioner in Palestine, Sir Herbert Samuel, wrote to the Secretary of State for the Colonies pointing out that the demands of the Najdi delegation meant evicting Transjordan from all of Wādī al-Sarhan, that Transjordan would be severed from Iraq along its southern border, and that the air route was bound to cross over Najdi possessions. He also pointed out that this situation would affect Hejaz too, threatening the Hejaz railway line, and that King Hussein was determined to see al-Nufud as a buffer between him and Ibn Saud.[74]

Two days later, the deputy Foreign Secretary cabled Knox that he had been directed by the Secretary of State to inform the chairman of the Kuwait Conference and the British representative there that under no circumstances was he to allow Najd to realize its demands concerning the extension of its northern borders beyond 'Unaiza and the Syrian border; in other words, he was not to allow Transjordan to be severed from Iraq.[75]

When the twelfth and thirteenth sessions were held, respectively, on 21 and 22 January 1924, it became clear that the conference had reached a dead end. The Najdi and Iraqi delegations requested an adjournment in order to consult their governments over points of difference which had arisen. Knox declared that he had cabled the request to his government and, until he had word from that end, he could not allow either delegation to leave. Until that time, Knox had been hoping that King Hussein might still change his mind and decide to take part in the conference. He therefore added that, once again, he was also awaiting word from Hejaz regarding the view of its government, and word from the Jordanian delegation.

In a report to the Secretary of State for the Colonies dated 21 January 1924, Knox stated that since agreement had been reached between Iraq and Najd on all major issues except the return of the tribes which had sought refuge in Iraq, he saw no point in continuing with the negotiations, and that the two delegations needed to consult their governments for new instructions. Knox also pointed out that an adjournment of the conference until 5 March had been proposed; he would, however, prefer an adjournment until 24 February. He then felt that it would be useful if the Iraqi delegation remained until the Jordanian delegation returned in order to keep the conference alive. He would be writing to the Sultan of Najd to clarify the position of the Iraqi delegation on the issue of the tribes which had sought refuge in Iraq, and, on behalf of the Secretary of State for the Colonies, to put forward suggestions on this issue.[76]

With this in mind, Knox wrote to Imam Sultan Abdul-Aziz as follows:

> I believe that Your Majesty would find it appropriate to change or amend the instructions which you have issued to your representatives, in order to enable us to reach the desired aim, which is to establish general security and maintain order within the borders of Najd and Iraq. Agreement has been reached regarding all issues except that which relates to the return of the tribes which sought refuge in Iraq and over which marked differences remain.

Knox then proposed that each party undertake either to permit free movement, or to prevent tribes and individuals from crossing into or seeking refuge in the territory of the other. He mentioned that his proposal had come in a telegram from the Secretary of State for the Colonies. Outlining the Iraqi viewpoint, Knox explained that the huge extent of the Iraqi territory made it impossible to exclude refugees, and that the tribes which fled to Iraq did not do so collectively but in a piecemeal fashion. This made it impossible for Iraq to use its armed forces to combat infiltration. Furthermore, there was a lack of adequate funds and a general absence of the necessary arrangements, together with the difficulty of keeping soldiers constantly on the move in such a vast area.

Knox reiterated the Iraqi statement that were Iraq to expel these tribes, they would not go back to Najd, but would cross the border into Syria or Turkey instead and use these two countries to launch attacks on both Iraq and Najd. If this were to happen, the other neighbouring countries would ask of Iraq what Najd had asked, and Iraq would be exclusively preoccupied with this kind of problem.[77]

Following intensive efforts by the British High Commissioner in Jerusalem, King Hussein agreed to be represented by his son Emir Zaid, who was in Baghdad at the time. This was confirmed in telegrams which the High Commissioner sent to the Colonial Office, to the British Representative in Jiddah, to Baghdad and to Kuwait. The High Commissioner added that King Hussein was staying in Amman for a few more weeks. His first condition was that Sultan Abdul-Aziz must also send one of his sons to the conference to achieve a balance in the level of representation. Another condition was that negotiations were to be conducted on the basis of a return to the pre-war borders.[78]

The British High Commissioner in Iraq expressed satisfaction with the appointment of Emir Zaid as King Hussein's representative to the conference. Such a feeling emanated from the view expressed by King Feisal himself, namely that his brother Zaid would help in solving the border problems between Hejaz and Najd.[79]

Knox had by then received a reply from Imam Sultan Abdul-Aziz to his letter referred to above. The Imam pointed out that, in his opinion, the main issue was that of the criminal tribes which sought refuge in Iraq. Leaving that door open to the various tribes would only make it extremely difficult for him to punish aggressors who flouted the rules of Islam and local laws. Noting the King's reply, Knox wrote to the Secretary of State for the Colonies that the only solution was for the British government to send an official to meet with the Sultan of Najd, or for the Sultan to send one of his sons to represent him at the conference as a counterbalance to Emir Zaid, King Hussein's son.[80]

But in a letter to the Secretary of State for the Colonies dated 30 January 1924, Knox was not optimistic, complaining about the halting progress of the conference and of the general lack of a responsible attitude. He added that his state of health would not allow him to continue and that the effort which he had put in had caused him to suffer a relapse. In this letter, Knox put forward a number of alternatives: conclude the conference under the pretext of the chairman's illness; adjourn it until the following spring; or appoint someone else as chairman, making sure that another, more appropriate representative be added to the Najdi delegation.[81]

As for the British government's proposals concerning the northern borders of the Sultanate of Najd, Sultan Imam Abdul-Aziz insisted that what had been suggested by the Najdi delegates, namely that the Najdi borders extended to the Syrian border, was based on the understanding that the government of Transjordan was an independent government. The Sultan added that, as the border problems concerned the British government in its capacity as the mandating power, it would be possible for Najd and the British government to agree directly. The Sultan of Najd also insisted that he did not agree to the borders of Transjordan and Iraq remaining joined, for fear of the machinations which the rulers of these two countries were capable of, and because Najd did not want to see the government of Transjordan having a say in Najd's trade and vital resources.[82]

King Hussein's decision to send his son Emir Zaid as his representative to the Kuwait Conference was the outcome of a meeting in Amman between the King and the British High Commissioner for Palestine on 21 January 1924. The High Commissioner was accompanied by Sir Gilbert Clayton, Sir Ronald Storrs and Richmond. With the King were his son Emir Abdullah and his Foreign Minister, Sheikh Fuad al-Khatib. At the meeting, the High Commissioner stated that the aim of the Kuwait Conference was to settle the problems which had arisen between the various Arab countries. He expressed his hope that King Hussein would participate and pointed out that the goal of the British government was to settle these problems, and that the conference was an ideal opportunity to achieve such a goal.

King Hussein replied that he doubted neither Britain's good intentions, nor its honourable goal in convening the conference. However, he expressed his surprise at not being consulted in advance. He reminded the meeting that during the First World War Britain had striven to secure Arab assistance, offered him a role, and considered him to be the leader who could help Britain achieve its aims and who could speak on behalf of all the Arabs. Britain addressed the King as the leader of the Arab revolt against the Turks, thus fulfilling all the undertakings he had made. But why then, the King asked at this point, had Britain not consulted him before convening the Kuwait Conference? King Hussein added that had he been consulted, he would have advised against the idea of convening a conference, because he was well aware that the causes of the trouble were numerous and deep-rooted.[83]

King Hussein then started to explain how these causes could be traced back to what he called the ambition of the Sultan of Najd, and his seizure of many areas. The King claimed that the only solution lay in the return of these areas to the *status quo ante*. He promised that, if the British were to help in this, they would find in him a faithful ally who would closely bind Arab interests to those of Britain.

The High Commissioner replied that he hoped the King would not boycott the next phase of the conference. He pointed out that if the conference failed because of the non-participation of Hejaz, this would have disastrous consequences and create a bad impression. He tried to persuade the King that his participation in the conference would give him the opportunity to make his views known to all. King Hussein replied that if he were to take part in the conference, this would only mean that he was seeking to return to the *status quo* before the expansion of Najd. He would make this a condition for his participation in the negotiations and on this basis would send his son Zaid as his representative.

When commenting on the King's agreeing to participate in the negotiations and his encouragement of the conference, the High Commissioner said that such a move was prompted by the same motive which had previously prompted the King's selfless stance in declaring the Arab revolt and in the war. He concluded his description of the meeting by saying that at the end the King stood up in the middle of the room, pointed to a fireplace and said that the fire reminded him of his position in 1916 when he, his sons and his followers were saviours, risking life and limb and defying the horrors of war in response to a request by the British government.[84]

While the conference was in adjournment, Colonel Trevor, Britain's chief accredited Representative in the Gulf, wrote on 8 February 1924 to the Sultan of Najd, requesting him to send to the next phase of the conference someone of a higher rank than the present representatives and that, because of the chairman's illness, the conference had to be postponed. A month later, Trevor wrote to Imam Sultan Abdul-Aziz, urging him to send one of his sons, as King Hussein had decided to send his son to the conference as his representative. The Sultan, however, rejected this for a number of reasons, including the fact that the people and *ulema* of Najd did not agree to one of his sons shouldering this onerous responsibility and that he had already given the present representatives full powers to negotiate on all outstanding matters between Najd and Hejaz.[85]

The conference opened its third phase on 25 March 1924 in an atmosphere which was far from optimistic. The representatives of Hejaz and Iraq were not even present. Recalled by his government in protest at a raid launched, as the Iraqis claimed, by the Ikhwan on the border of Iraq, the

Iraqi representative had cut short his trip and returned to Baghdad from Basra, where he had just arrived on his way to Kuwait.

Thus, the negotiations in this session were restricted to the delegations of Najd and Transjordan. The latter reiterated its demands for the return of al-Jof, Sakaka and Wādī al-Sarhan and insisted on its original proposals. In fact, the Jordanians went further than this in demanding the return of the Emirate of Hā'il, and the reinstating of the 'Ayid family in 'Asīr.[86]

In February 1924 an event occurred which opened the way for a conflict that was new not only to the Arab world, but to the Islamic world as a whole: Mustafa Kemal announced the abolition of the Caliphate. King Hussein reacted by attacking the Kuwait Conference and using his tough stance against Britain to redeem himself for his past errors in the eyes of the Islamic world. He thought that the British could not land their troops in Hejaz, and he was nursing dreams of being the future Caliph. This led him to declare that Feisal and Abdullah were merely his deputies in Iraq and Transjordan.[87] It was then that Britain decided to close the Kuwait Conference, which thus ended in failure.

5
Results of the Kuwait Conference

Analysis of Previous Chapters

In Chapter 1, we followed the establishment of the Sultanate of Najd and its Dependencies and concluded with the emergence of the border problems, which were varied, and which grew as the newly emerging state developed in the hands of Imam King Abdul-Aziz, who regained what had belonged to his forefathers. In the second section of the chapter, we clarified the nature of these problems, particularly those relating to the various tribes and clans and their movement in areas which had never known political borders.

As made abundantly clear, the aim of the discussion in Chapter 2 on *al-Ashrāf* and the First World War, as well as on the Sherif Hussein–McMahon contacts, was to clarify the results of the war from the perspective of extending *al-Ashrāf* rule to Iraq and Transjordan under the mandate, a system which was one of the general outcomes of the war.

The discussion in Chapter 3 necessarily entailed a description of the attitude of the Ottoman Empire to the establishment and expansion of the Sultanate of Najd. Nor could we have ignored the attitude of Britain, which at the time was extremely influential in the Gulf, was an ally of King Hussein in Hejaz, and was the mandating power in Iraq, Transjordan and Palestine. This meant that Britain, albeit indirectly, was surrounding the new state.

The conclusions to be drawn from the exposition in the preceding chapters all point to the inevitability of convening the Kuwait Conference. As Chapter 3 drew to a close, we felt that we had treated this point adequately, paving the way for the discussion in Chapter 4 of the Kuwait Conference itself. In Chapter 4, we have shed adequate light on the important issues and problems which the conference addressed, as well as on the conference itself through its numerous sessions, and in its three phases.

The Results of the Kuwait Conference

In saying that the Kuwait Conference was abandoned and that it failed, we mean that it did not fulfil Britain's aspirations, as discussed exhaustively in the previous chapters. But the conference was also the platform which revealed a stark truth that was to become clear only when the conference was actually convened. In other words, it manifested a significant and critical shift which was to be appreciated only as it unfolded.

The Kuwait Conference was the mirror which reflected this truth and this shift, and Imam Abdul-Aziz perceived this with perspicacity. This perception had to be followed by the decision which the Imam took with the daring and determination for which his ancestors were renowned, and which had been characteristic of him ever since the very first step he took on the path to regaining what had always belonged to him and his forebears.

Although Britain was fighting the Turks during the First World War, and although circumstances were conducive to dealing the western part of the land (i.e. Hejaz) a sudden blow similar to that which had successfully been dealt to the east (i.e. 'Asīr), the descendant of the Al Saud wisely saw fit to exercise patience and to wait until that shift and that truth to which we referred above were fully revealed.

It is true that, before the First World War, in the eyes of supporters of Arab nationalism, King Hussein was a symbol of the hope for the establishment of an independent Arab state. But what happened after the war only revealed how false these hopes were. As has been pointed out, many Arab countries suffered under military occupation by Britain and France, and under two mandates (one British, the other French) in Iraq, Transjordan and Syria, while Palestine was promised to the Jews. Throughout all this, whether under occupation or under a mandate, King Hussein's two sons ruled.

An examination of the various official documents reveals Britain's keen desire that the Kuwait Conference be convened and be successful. The ultimate aim was, of course, to achieve global aims which came to be essential in the aftermath of the First World War. The conference failed simply because of the antagonism King Hussein showed towards it, insisting that he would not send a representative. However, when British pressure increased, urging him to co-operate in the final phase, the King decided to send his son, Emir Zaid. But this was not without conditions laid down by the King and which made his late participation in the conference as harmful as his previous boycott. Thus, in the end, it was Britain's most trusted ally who undermined the conference. The British deeply regretted the failure of the conference, and were only too aware that it was their ally King Hussein who had frustrated their peace efforts, while Sultan Abdul-Aziz had acted in a civilized, peace-loving manner.

Hussein was oblivious to Britain's advice on the need to improve his relations with his neighbours, particularly the Sultanate of Najd. Despite Britain's efforts to persuade the King to take part in the conference, he insisted on his condition that Ibn Saud relinquish all the land which he had regained in recent years, and return to the pre-1919 borders. It was then that Britain realized that it was dealing with an intractable situation and that the King was making demands as if he were the victorious party.

Britain also realized how dangerous the insistence of the Iraqi and Jordanian delegations was in the last phase of the conference when they declared that their agreement with the Sultanate of Najd was suspended until differences between the Sultanate and Hejaz were settled.

Hussein's failure to recognize the new developments in the region in the aftermath of the First World War meant that he continued to insist on giving al-Jof and Wādī al-Sarhan to the Emirate of Transjordan, and on the return of Taima', Khaibar, Turba and al-Kharma to Hejaz. His intransigence went further than this: he insisted that the Rashīd family be restored to Hā'il and al-'Ayid to 'Asīr.

Imam Sultan Abdul-Aziz was watching developments at the Kuwait Conference from al-Ihsā'. He was soon convinced that the neighbouring rulers did not wish him well. He believed that, with the regimes in Iraq, Transjordan and Hejaz collaborating to thwart the prosperity and progress of Najd, there would be no stability. This was made abundantly clear by the behaviour of the Iraqi and Jordanian delegations, the attitude of Hejaz *vis-à-vis* the conference, and the demands of these three parties, as well as by the way the negotiations were going.

Furthermore, a few years had elapsed since Hussein had prevented the Najdis from performing the *haj*, under the pretext of the Saudi occupation of Turba and al-Kharma and the fear that there would be clashes between the Najdis and followers of other movements. Imam Abdul-Aziz remembered that it was the British who had forced him to retreat from the Hejaz border in 1919, a period in which Hussein was their obedient ally. But the Kuwait Conference was to reveal something new: Hussein had now become an opponent of Britain and it was his intransigence which had undermined the conference on which Britain had pinned all its hopes in the Arab region.

The conference clearly demonstrated the impossibility of Najd's co-existing with Hejaz, and that no alternative was left but the sword. It was inconceivable that Britain would continue to protect its former ally, and it was thus unlikely that Hussein would be as obstructive as he had been in 1919. It was as though the Kuwait Conference, having failed to achieve a settlement, establish stability in the Arab region and realize Britain's objectives, had nevertheless been successful in creating and revealing this significant change in the situation.

Najd thus moved against Hejaz.

The Annexation of Hejaz—the Hejazi Kingdom

We have already referred to the abolition of the Caliphate by Mustafa Kemal in February 1924, a development which made King Hussein eagerly and hastily, and in a most conspicuous and confrontational manner, declare himself Caliph—a position to which many Islamic leaders were aspiring—the following month. The self-appointed Caliph was on a visit to Amman at the time, when he announced that his sons in Iraq and Transjordan were his deputies.[1]

With King Fuad of Egypt himself aspiring to the Caliphate, Egyptian public opinion and the al-Azhar *ulema* were up in arms. Imam Sultan Abdul-Aziz found the opposition of the Islamic world to King Hussein's assumption of the Caliphate an ideal opportunity to lay the groundwork for his future battles with Hejaz. The Indian Muslims hated King Hussein for his stance towards the Ottoman Empire in the First World War. This hatred increased when he declared himself Caliph. The Turkish Caliphate Society was to carry the banner of the opposition.[2] For its part, France sought to turn the situation to its own advantage by encouraging the Sultan of Morocco to become Caliph, which would tip the balance in the Islamic world in France's favour.

As soon as Ankara announced that it was abandoning the Caliphate, both Emir Abdullah and his father decided to try to use the event to enhance the glory of their family, and to counteract the supremacy of Ibn Saud. The aim was to make the British see the urgency of the situation. An *ad hoc* meeting was held in the village of al-Shona near Amman, at which King Hussein was declared Caliph. Britain viewed this measure as a challenge to its authority, and this feeling was compounded by the concern with and influence of the Indian Muslims,[3] and by the revelations which emerged at the Kuwait Conference. Sultan Abdul-Aziz decided to march on Hejaz.

It is perhaps worth noting at this point that the movement of annexation and reclamation which Imam Sultan Abdul-Aziz had embarked on was similar to that of the conquest of the first Saudi state.[4] In 1924 a conference had been convened in Riyadh attended by all the clan chieftains, *ulema* and tribesmen and by Abdul-Aziz himself. The conference was presided over by Abdul-Aziz's father, Imam Abdul-Rahman, who opened it by saying that he had received many petitions stating the desire of his fellow Muslims to perform the *haj*. Those in attendance confirmed that the *haj* was one of the five pillars of Islam, that Mecca was not the property of King Hussein, that the King had no right to prevent Muslims from fulfilling this duty and that this ban justified the Najdis in invading Hejaz.

Imam Sultan Abdul-Aziz explained that the Sherif of Mecca had not responded positively to the attempts to solve the problems between Najd and Hejaz. (This was a reference to the Kuwait Conference.) At this point, the audience began to chant 'For Hejaz', and the religio-legal verdict was thus issued.[5]

The conference concluded with a statement signed by Emir Feisal bin Abdul-Aziz al-Saud. The statement mentioned that King Hussein had been preventing the people of Najd from performing the *haj* for more than three years, using the excuse of not wishing Najdis to clash with Muslim followers of the other schools of thought. The truth, however, was that he was afraid that the call for unity would spread and sweep across Hejaz.[6]

A huge Saudi force advanced from Turba. The Ikhwan army comprised 15 brigades and consisted of nearly 3,000 fighters who came from all over Najd and its Dependencies; all the tribes were represented. The Saudi army arrived at al-Hawiyya, a few kilometres from Taif. Engagements took place just outside Taif, including the Hawiyya battle and the battle of Taif. The Hashemite army was defeated. With the Saudi army using the element of surprise most effectively, together with speed of movement, zeal, valour and single-mindedness, a breach was finally opened in the new Hashemite defence line at Huda. The Saudi army halted at Taif and Huda and awaited instructions from Imam Sultan Abdul-Aziz, who was still in Riyadh, to advance to Mecca. Meanwhile the Hashemites withdrew to Jiddah.

King Hussein abdicated and departed to Aqaba in 1924 and his son Ali bin Hussein came to power as King of Hejaz. Ali took Jiddah as a base and undertook to have it garrisoned. Politically, he was inclined to reach an understanding with Sultan Abdul-Aziz and to work towards persuading the British to seek a reconciliation pact with the Sultan and to use the good offices of his followers to secure his endorsement of such a pact.[7] But developments at the Kuwait Conference, and Britain's repeated failure to involve Hejaz, all rendered the King's endeavours in this direction futile.

While on his way to Mecca, in November 1924, Imam Abdul-Aziz received a letter carried by Sultan Ibn Bijad and signed by all accredited Consuls in Jiddah, including most prominently the British Representative. The letter was addressed to the generals of the Saudi armies in Mecca, informing them that the undersigned and their governments adhered to a position of neutrality as far as the war between the Saudis and the Hashemites was concerned. It was at this moment that Abdul-Aziz was reassured that he had been right all along in his conclusions concerning the Kuwait Conference and subsequent events. He was particularly pleased with the shift in the British position. Britain had once warned him to cease fire after the battle of Turba in 1918; it was now neutral.[8]

One can perhaps discern a slowing down of the advance to Mecca after the taking of Taif. This was to enable Imam Abdul-Aziz to assess the various reactions to his move. But now that Britain's neutral position was clear, the Saudi troops continued to push on. (What had persuaded Britain to opt for neutrality was King Hussein's attitude towards the Kuwait Conference.) The Imam's mounted escort arrived in Mecca in December 1924.

The following day, a well-attended reception was held in honour of Imam Abdul-Aziz at al-Abtah. The Imam spoke about his aims in entering Hejaz and explained the plans he intended to pursue in the Hejazi lands. The following evening, he met with the *ulema* of Mecca to tell them the real truth about the Najdis and their doctrine. At this meeting, which took place at the Hamidiyya reception hall, the Imam invited those present to adhere to the Qur'ān and asked them to swear to act justly in accordance with this holy book, the traditions of the Prophet and of the wise Caliphs after him.

An announcement was made to all town-dwellers and bedouin in and around Mecca, which included the following statement:

> We have left our homeland to come to you only to stand up for the religion of God, whose sanctity has been violated, and to fend off the evils which have been plotted against us and our homeland by those who have behaved tyrannically against you and against us.
>
> The source of jurisprudence can be derived only from the Book of God, from the traditions of the Prophet and from what has been endorsed by the Muslims through *qiyās* [analogical reasoning][9] and the consensus of opinion. It is only the weak whom I consider as great until I regain for them what is rightful; and it is only the unjust whom I consider as weak until I regain from them what is rightful. In applying the rules of God I

> know no compromise and I accept no intermediaries. The unjust shall only blame themselves. God be my witness.[10]

A few days later, the Hashemite forces in al-Madīnah surrendered, as did all the ports and villages which lay within its area.[11] Jiddah was besieged for nearly ten months. King Ali bin Hussein left the city for Iraq on 16 December 1925. On 24 December, Imam Sultan Abdul-Aziz finally entered Jiddah.[12]

Before King Ali's departure and Sultan Abdul-Aziz's entering Jiddah, the Sultan had been preparing to take Aqaba and expel King Hussein, who was providing the Hashemites in Jiddah with assistance. Faced with this threat, King Hussein left Aqaba for Cyprus. The King's departure was prompted by a warning which the British government relayed to the King through the armoured cruiser HMS *Cornflower*, which was docked in Aqaba at the time. The memorandum read as follows:

> To King Hussein, from the Deputy Minister of the Foreign Office of Great Britain,
>
> The Government of Great Britain has learnt that the Sultan of Najd has prepared a force to attack Aqaba where the government of Your Majesty is at the moment. His Majesty's government therefore urges you to leave Aqaba so as not to become the cause of new problems between Britain and the Sultan of Najd.

The King was then told that he must leave for Cyprus; his role in the area thus came to an end.[13]

Alternatives to the Positions of the Kuwait Conference—the Border Problems

With the abdication of King Hussein and his departure from Hejaz, the way was being gradually paved for what may be called the alternatives to the positions of the Kuwait Conference. By alternatives are meant those conditions which were conducive to the bilateral settlement of problems between Iraq and Najd, and between Najd and Transjordan.

An agreement was concluded between Najd and Iraq at Bahra,[14] which included the following statement and articles:

> Noting the treaty concluded at al-Muhammara on 5 May 1922 between the government of Iraq and the government of Najd with the aim of promoting good relations between them,

Further noting the two protocols known as protocol no. 1 and protocol no. 2 which were signed at al-'Uqair on 2 December 1922 and which were appended to the above-mentioned treaty,

Bearing in mind the belief of both governments and that of His Majesty's British government that, out of concern for friendly relations between Iraq and Najd, it was desirable for these two countries to conclude an agreement concerning the settlement of outstanding issues between them,

The undersigned, the Sultan of Najd and its Dependencies, Abdul-Aziz bin Abdul Rahman al-Feisal al-Saud, Sir Gilbert Clayton, the plenipotentiary representative of the Iraqi government, have agreed on the following:

Article I

The state of Iraq and the state of Najd recognize that raids by tribes settled in the territories of one party on the territories of the other party are acts of aggression whose perpetrators must be severely punished by the government concerned, and with the chieftain of the aggressive clan held personally responsible.[15]

Article II

a. A special tribunal to deal with issues arising from this agreement between Iraq and Najd shall be constituted and shall meet from time to time to look into details of any act of aggression taking place behind the borders of either country, and to calculate the losses and damages incurred and assign the responsibility. The tribunal shall consist of an equal number of representatives from both parties and shall be presided over by someone other than these representatives, to be chosen by both governments. The decisions of the tribunal shall be final and implementable.

....

Article III

The clans of each party may only cross the border of the other after obtaining permission from their own government and after securing the agreement of the other government, bearing in mind that neither government has the right to withhold such permission or such agreement if the reason for a particular clan's movement is to search for grazing land in accordance with the grazing law.

Article VI included the following clause:

> The forces of each party shall go beyond their own border in chasing criminals only with the consent of the two governments.

Article X included the following clause:

> The two governments undertake to hold friendly discussions concerned with concluding a special agreement for the extradition of criminals in accordance with what is customary between friendly countries and within a period of a year from the date of ratifying this agreement by the government of Iraq.[16]

Appended to this treaty was the correspondence between Sultan Abdul-Aziz and General Clayton regarding outstanding issues of loot claimed by either party.

Then an agreement between Najd and Transjordan was concluded. The preamble included the following statement and articles:

> Noting the relations existing between the Exalted government of Britain, on the one hand, and the Sultanate of Najd and its Dependencies, on the other,
>
> Desiring to demarcate the borders between Najd and Transjordan, and to settle outstanding issues related to the border question,
>
> The Exalted British government has appointed Sir Gilbert Clayton a plenipotentiary representative to conclude an agreement in this respect with Sultan Abdul-Aziz bin Abdul Rahman al-Feisal al-Saud on behalf of Najd:
>
> *Article I*
> The north-eastern border between Najd and Transjordan shall begin at the point of intersection of longitude 39° east and latitude 32° north, at which point the border between Najd and Iraq ends on a straight line until the point of intersection of longitude 37° east and latitude 30–31° north and thus follows longitude 37° north. It then extends on a straight line to the point of the intersection of longitude 38° east and latitude 30° north, leaving for Najd those parts of Wādī al-Sarhan which are visible.
>
> *Article II*
> The government of Najd undertakes not to establish a garrison in Qaf, and not to use this and the adjacent area as a military zone. Furthermore,

the government shall undertake by all available means to prevent its forces from committing any act of aggression against Transjordan.

Article III

To prevent any misunderstanding likely to result from incidents occurring near the borders, to strengthen bonds of mutual trust between the two parties, and to achieve total co-operation between His Majesty's British government and the government of Najd, the two parties agree that close contact be maintained between the British Representative in Transjordan or his deputy and the ruler of Wādī al-Sarhan.[17]

Article IV

The government of Najd undertakes to protect all the inalienable rights enjoyed by all the non-Najdi tribes in Wādī al-Sarhan, whether these rights concern grazing, domicile, ownership or similar rights, on condition that these tribes abide by the internal laws of Najd, which do not infringe these rights, as long as they are in Najdi lands. The government of Transjordan shall similarly treat Najdi nationals who enjoy similar inalienable rights in Transjordan.

Article V

Najd and Transjordan recognize that raids by clans settled in the territories of one party on those of the other constitute an act of aggression whose perpetrators shall be severely punished by the government of the aggressor clan, and that the chief of the clan shall be held personally responsible for such violations.

Article VI

a. A special tribunal shall be constituted by agreement between the two governments of Najd and Transjordan, which shall meet from time to time to look into the details of any aggression taking place within the borders of each party, and to calculate the losses and damages and assign the responsibility for such acts.

Article IX included the following clause:

The governments of Najd and Transjordan may not communicate with the heads and chiefs of each other's clans on official and political matters.

Article X included the following clause:

> The forces of Najd and those of Transjordan may not go beyond each other's borders with the intention of tracking down criminals without the prior consent of the two governments.

Article XII contained the following clause:

> The governments of Najd and Transjordan shall accord all travellers and pilgrims the right to free passage.[18]

Article XIII, which dealt with Najd's demands concerning its trade with Syria, included the following statement:

> His Majesty's British government undertakes to secure free passage to and from Najd and Syria at all times for Najdi merchants to go about their business, and that they are entitled to exemption from customs duties and other taxes on all goods passing through the mandated area on their way from Najd to Syria or from Syria to Najd. This is on condition that these traders and their caravans comply with the necessary customs inspection and carry proper documentation from their own governments testifying to their legal status (as traders), and that trade caravans carrying goods shall follow known routes, to be subsequently determined, for entering into or exiting from the mandated areas, bearing in mind that these restrictions shall not apply to caravans which restrict their trading to camels and animals, or to clans which move about in accordance with the preceding articles of this treaty.

This treaty was followed by an exchange of correspondence between the Sultan of Najd and its Dependencies and General Clayton regarding the interpretation of Article II, which concerned the garrisoning of Qaf, and relating to Transjordan's merchants and their use of the Wādī al-Sarhan route.[19]

Reference has already been made to Sultan Abdul-Aziz's entry into Mecca and his speech at al-Abtah, as well as the communiqué addressed to the Hejazis who lived in and around Mecca. The freeing and annexation of Hejaz was received with jubilation by the entire Islamic world.[20] *Al-Balagh*, a newspaper which was then published in Alexandria, commented on the Sultan's speech as follows:

> With this message, the Sultan of Najd goes to Umm al-Qura. God and the people shall testify that he was a man who never hesitated to put into action what he appropriately intended to do. What a noble aim he was

> pursuing, and who better qualified to receive the endorsement of the entire Islamic world in carrying out this formidable task with which he was entrusted by destiny. The Sultan's tone reminds us all of that of the worthy ancestors, the venerable forefathers. His conduct, rectitude and strength of belief reassure and comfort all of us Muslims.[21]

The first pilgrimage to be performed under the call for unity and reform and which took place in 1925 was the best testimony to the falsehood of the rumours that had previously been spread by Ottoman dignitaries and officials about this call.[22] It may even be said that the regaining of Riyadh and the annexation of the other areas which were to comprise the Sultanate of Najd and its Dependencies did not make as strong an impact on the Islamic world as that of the Saudi army's advance into Hejaz. As the location of the two holy shrines of Mecca and al-Madīnah, Hejaz occupied a distinctive place both for Muslims and internationally.[23]

After he had liberated Hejaz, Sultan Abdul-Aziz wished to convene an Islamic conference in Mecca in order to enable the Muslims to elect a ruler who took his lead from the Islamic world and was guided only by the Islamic nations. This move reassured the Islamic world that the Sultan was not intent on devouring Hejaz but, rather, wished to pay back those who behaved badly towards him as well as to demonstrate the validity of the Salafi call.

The *ulema* of Mecca had asked the Sultan to arrange a meeting between them and the *ulema* of Najd to discuss the sources and applications of Islamic law. The Sultan agreed and a meeting was arranged at which a number of Meccan *ulema* met seven *ulema* from Najd. The meeting deliberated in depth, and at the conclusion of the debate the Meccan *ulema* issued a statement which included the following avowal:

> The *ulema* of Najd and ourselves have agreed on the question of the sources. In matters of the faith, we, the *ulema* of Mecca and our brothers in Najd, are in agreement.[24]

The idea of an Islamic Conference in Mecca to determine the fate of Hejaz was later to crystallize. The aid which Hejaz received from the other Islamic nations had a significant role to play, but the Hejazis rejected the suggestion made by the Indian Caliphate Society that Hejaz should be placed under a joint administration of all Islamic nations. To the Hejazis this meant that the land would be ruled by outsiders and Hejaz would be ruled at the whim of foreigners via representatives of countries already under foreign domination. They thus called for Hejaz to be for the Hejazis and stated that the Hejazis and their Najdi brethren were equals.[25]

Results of the Kuwait Conference

There was unanimity in declaring allegiance to Abdul-Aziz and proclaiming him King of Hejaz, with Mecca as its capital. This was declared on 10 January 1926. Imam Sultan Abdul-Aziz thus became 'King of Hejaz and the Sultan of Najd and its Dependencies'.[26]

When asked about the constitution, the King replied, 'Our constitution is the holy Qur'ān.' The state, however, had its first system laid down on the basis of King Abdul-Aziz's principles, which he dictated in Mecca in September 1926. A commission known as the General Assembly was charged with formulating the various articles, which were then published in the official gazette under the title, 'New Regulations for the Hejazi Kingdom'.

In these regulations, the head of the Hejaz government was named, relations between Najd and Hejaz were defined, the flag and currency were determined, consultative councils were established for all towns, and a General Consultative Council was constituted to include members elected by the local consultative councils. The Basic Regulations comprised 79 articles in 9 parts.

The preamble of the Regulations stated:

> These Basic Regulations are issued by royal endorsement in September 1926. Part I includes: the Kingdom, the Form of the State, the Capital, and the Official Language. This is in four articles.

Part II included 'the Administration of the Kingdom, Laws, Public Prosecution, the Responsibilities of the Administration'. Part III dealt with a number of issues concerning the Hejazi Kingdom.[27]

Having considered Part IV of the Basic Regulations, King Abdul-Aziz issued an amendment which was in effect a new system for the General Consultative Council. The new system stipulated that the council, presided over by the Public Prosecutor,[28] was to consist of eight members, four of whom would be selected by the government in its own capacity, with two of these being from Najd, and another four also selected by the government but after consultation with those outside the government with sufficient knowledge and experience.

The annexation of Hejaz thus required hasty arrangements to be made in line with the conditions prevalent in Hejaz at the time and in the light of the call for unity and reform. The annexation of Hejaz also led to the recognition of the new kingdom by the outside world. This was enshrined in the Mecca agreement, concluded between Hejaz, Najd, and France as the representative of Syria. The preamble of the agreement included the following statement:

> The French government has chosen al-Sherif Ibrahim, deputized by Monsieur Henri de Jouvenel, member of the French Senate and the French High Commissioner to the governments of Syria and Lebanon, and appointed him a plenipotentiary representative to sign a trade agreement with His Majesty the King of Hejaz and Najd and its Dependencies.

Article I, paragraphs a, b and c, regulated the customs system. Article II included the following clause: 'Najdi tribes shall deposit their arms with the police station in the town which they enter in return for a receipt. These arms shall be returned to their owners when they leave the town.' Article II dealt with gold. Article IV tackled legal issues. Article V, paragraphs a and b, regulated the movement of tribes and was signed by 'His Majesty King of Hejaz and the Sultan of Najd and its Dependencies'.[29]

The Annexation of 'Asīr

The Turks had prepared a plan to fight Muhammad al-Idrisi in 'Asīr in 1902: this was to besiege him from the north and south by a force led by Feisal bin Hussein of Mecca, and from San'ā' and al-Lahya by another Ottoman force. But when this plan failed, the Ottoman forces held on to the coast of 'Asīr from Lahya to Zahran as protection for al-Hudaida. The Turks began to lure Feisal bin Hussein with the Emirate of 'Asīr as reward if he succeeded in defeating the Idrisi. Al-Idrisi's resistance to the Ottomans increased after their reconciliation with the Imam of Yemen.[30]

When Italy declared war against the Ottoman Empire in 1911 and began the occupation of Tripoli, it turned towards the Red Sea and besieged the *vilayet* of Yemen. The Italian fleet anchored off Jīzān to enable al-Idrisi to descend from his mountain retreat, make contact with them and receive supplies of arms.

When the First World War broke out, Muhammad al-Idrisi was the first to respond to the call of the British, with whom he was later to conclude a treaty in 1915. When he died in 1923, he was succeeded by his son Ali. But the Idrisi family was torn by internal feuds. Ali bin Muhammad al-Idrisi entered into negotiations with the Italians in Massawa. He also negotiated with the British in Aden, granting them concessionary rights to extract oil from the Fursan Islands. Furthermore, al-Idrisi persuaded Imam Yahya of Yemen to cease advancing into Tihama.

During the era of Imam Saud the Great, the call for unity and reform became widespread and was accepted by the people of the region. This, however, left them vulnerable to the attacks of the Ottoman Empire, and later to the oppression of Muhammad Ali. It was for this reason that the Idrisi concluded a treaty with King Abdul-Aziz in 1926, in accordance with which they left what remained of their kingdom under his protection.[31]

The history of the relations between Najd and Yemen goes back to the time when the borders of these two lands merged as a result of the merger of 'Asīr province with Najd (1921–22). When the Mecca treaty was concluded between King Abdul-Aziz and al-Sayyid al-Hasan bin Ali al-Idrisi on 21 October 1926, the former extended his control over that part of Tihama which was governed by the Idrisi.[32]

King Hussein persisted in stirring up Banu Shahr, who lived in Abha, encouraging them to unite with the 'Ayid family against Ibn Saud, and supplying them with funds and arms. But Emir Feisal bin Abdul-Aziz was able to occupy Abha and defeat the force which King Hussein had sent to Tihama. He was also able to restore the Emirate to Ibn 'Ufaisan in January 1923. Even when King Hussein's kingdom was disintegrating, he looked to the Idrisi and 'Asīr, seeking the assistance of the Shafi'is in Yemen.[33]

While Imam Sultan Abdul-Aziz was preoccupied with the liberation of Hejaz, Imam Yahya made a move to extend his control over the 'Asīr Emirate, which was considered as under Saudi protection since 1920. Imam Yahya annexed Najrān, which was an inviolable zone between the two countries. But no sooner had the Saudi forces achieved victory at al-Kharma than they hastened to put an end to Yemeni threats. Yemen had to withdraw from Najrān, and the above-mentioned Mecca treaty with the Idrisi was concluded. The annexation of Hejaz was a crucial factor in consolidating Saudi rule in 'Asīr. When the Saudi forces subsequently entered al-Hudaida, British, French and Italian naval forces appeared off the coast with the intention of intervening. The Saudis stopped short of entering San'ā' and King Abdul-Aziz, a seasoned observer of peninsular history, decided not to occupy Yemen.[34]

King Hussein was striving to establish what he called the Shafi'i Emirate, whose borders he envisaged as follows. The lands populated by the Zaidis and that of the Shafi'is were to be separated by the lofty mountains of Naqīl Samāra. From the Idrisi side, the lands that were ruled by al-Idrisi were to be separated by the area extending from the start of Bait al-Faqīh. From the side of the Lahaj Emirate, the border was to commence from the start of Bilad al-Hawashib. Finally, from the shore of the Red Sea, the border was to be the administrative district of Mecca, which King Hussein envisaged as the commercial port, with Ta'iz as the capital of this Shafi'i Emirate.

King Hussein declared that the Sultanates of Lahaj, Hadramawt, Ibbin and al-'Awāliq and the surrounding Emirates and Sheikhdoms should all be under the new Emirate instead of under the Protecting State. Together with the King's stance on the Kuwait Conference, this vision of future developments angered Britain. King Hussein made it a condition that the new Emirate would recognize his flag as its own, that its currency would bear his own name as King of the Arabs, and that it would use the stamps of the Hejazi postal service.[35] But in the wake of the failure of the Kuwait Conference, the annexation of Hejaz seemed to have put paid to all these dreams.

It was obvious that none of the countries which the Sultanate of Hejaz, Najd and its Dependencies was to comprise had previously known foreign political representation. Thus, one of Imam King Abdul-Aziz's first projects after entering Hejaz was to organize international relations between his country and other nations. Gone were the days when individuals intervened in an unofficial capacity; the time had now come for Ambassadors, Consuls and Plenipotentiary Ministers, whose point of reference was the Ministry of Foreign Affairs. The King also began to establish political and consular institutions with Arab and foreign governments.[36]

King Abdul-Aziz also embarked on the organization of the health sector, establishing the Public Health Board based in Mecca, with branches in Jiddah, al-Madīnah, Riyadh, al-Ihsā' and 'Asīr. At the beginning of the Saudi era in Hejaz, a Ports Authority was also established, which later became the Coastguard Directorate, based in Jiddah. Linking the various parts of this nascent expansive state to one another with a radio network was also felt to be essential.[37]

In the *haj* season of 1926, the whole Islamic world began to appreciate the importance of the new arrangements made by the Saudi government to secure pilgrims' lives and possessions. When the Egyptian Foreign Ministry requested that the leader of the pilgrimage be accompanied by entire battalions and their complements, and that this force come with a richly decorated litter, King Abdul-Aziz replied on 20 May 1926 that what was ordered by God and His Prophet should be implemented, thus denouncing the idea of the litter and the accompanying loud music. The Ikhwan and the people of Najd saw the litter as *bid'a* (unorthodox innovations). This incident took place on the first day of the 'Id al-Adha' and led to a clash between the Najdis and the Egyptians accompanying the litter. King Abdul-Aziz ordered that the troops accompanying the litter be stripped of their arms and that the display be banned in the Holy Shrine.[38]

The preamble of the Mecca agreement between King Abdul-Aziz and al-Idrisi included the following statement and articles:

His Majesty the King of Hejaz and Sultan of Najd and its Dependencies, Abdul-Aziz bin Abdul Rahman al-Feisal al-Saud,

and

His Excellency the Imam of 'Asīr, al-Sayyid al-Hasan bin Ali al-Idrisi,

Desiring to present a unified front,

Wishing to preserve the integrity of the Arab nation, [and]

Seeking to strengthen relations between the Emirs of the Arabian peninsula,

Have agreed on the following:

Article I

His Excellency Imam al-Sayyid al-Hasan bin Ali al-Idrisi recognizes that the old borders which are described in the agreement of 25 October 1920 concluded between the Sultan of Najd and Imam al-Sayyid Muhammad bin Ali al-Idrisi, and which were under the Idrisi at that time, are now under His Majesty the King of Hejaz and Sultan of Najd and its Dependencies.

....

Article IV

The Imam of 'Asīr may not relinquish any part of the lands of 'Asīr described in Article I.

....

Article VI

The King of Hejaz and Sultan of Najd and its Dependencies recognizes that the internal administration of the land of 'Asīr and the affairs of its clans regarding appointments, dismissals and other internal matters are the responsibility of the Imam of 'Asīr, provided that regulations are instituted in accordance with Islamic law and justice as is the case for both governments.

....

Article VII

The King of Hejaz and Sultan of Najd and its Dependencies undertakes to deter any internal or external act of aggression on the lands of 'Asīr described in Article I.[39]

Later, a meeting was held in Riyadh attended by all who held positions of power and influence. The meeting decided to transform the Sultanate of Najd and its Dependencies into a Kingdom, to be called the Kingdom of Najd and its Dependencies; the title 'King of Hejaz, Najd and its Dependencies' was adopted as of 19 January 1927.[40]

Treaties Following the Annexation of Hejaz

After the annexation of Hejaz, Sultan Abdul-Aziz decided that an Islamic Conference should be held in Mecca to agree on the means necessary to ensure the comfort of pilgrims. The conference, which opened on 7 June 1926, later resolved that Mecca should reclaim the Hejaz railway line, that the line be extended to link Mecca and Jiddah to al-Madīnah, and that all necessary steps be taken to ensure the health, comfort and wellbeing of the pilgrims and safeguard their possessions.

The conference also discussed the right of Hejaz to Aqaba and Ma'n on the grounds that these were Hejazi lands which Ali bin Hussein had relinquished to his brother Abdullah, the Emir of Transjordan.[41] Among the most important consequences of the conference were the recognition of Hejaz by the entire Islamic world, the demonstration of the truth of the Salafi call, and the start of the restoration of Hejaz. New regulations were introduced as appropriate and, once approved by Imam King Abdul-Aziz, were published in the semi-official newspaper, *Umm al-Qura*. Important regulations were those relating to the *haj*, the Council for Education and the General Police Authority (later known as the General Security Administration). The system of justice was also reorganized and based in Mecca.[42]

The restoration programme also included the means to combat feuds and lawlessness among the various tribes, to promote knowledge and self-improvement, and to inspire a cultural movement through the publication and distribution of books. There were numerous and varied reforms in both Mecca and al-Madīnah. Roads were constructed and public transport was made available, encouraging Muslims from all over the world to visit Hejaz in large numbers.

It is worth noting that a conference held in Cairo at the same time to confirm King Fuad as the Muslim Caliph ended in failure. King Abdul-Aziz had already made clear his position on the Caliphate, saying that he was too unworldly to be preoccupied with titles and that neither he, his family or his Kingdom wished to be dragged into feuds and contentious issues.[43]

King Abdul-Aziz was constantly thinking of how to dispense with the 'Uqair protocols, signed with Britain (represented by its accredited Agent in the Arabian Gulf, Sir Percy Cox) on 26 December 1915. For its part, Britain also felt that the time had come to abandon the protocols, given the historical transformation which the region was undergoing at the hands of Imam Abdul-Aziz, who now controlled the two routes to India, via the Gulf and the Red Sea. Britain thus decided to send a delegation headed by Sir Gilbert Clayton to negotiate amendments to the 1915 treaty. The negotiations also broached the issue of foreign concessions which had been valid for Hejaz when this was an Ottoman *vilayet*, the issue of Aqaba and Ma'n, and the issue of slavery and the inspection of ships.

The Jiddah agreement was finally concluded between the British Empire and the King of Hejaz, Najd and its Dependencies. The preamble included the following statement and articles:

> We, Abdul-Aziz bin Abdul Rahman al-Feisal al-Saud, King of Hejaz, Najd and its Dependencies,
>
> Having concluded a Treaty of Friendship and Understanding with His Majesty the King of Great Britain, Ireland, the British Colonies overseas and the Empire of India,
>
> Have agreed to the following:
>
> His Majesty the King of Great Britain, Ireland, the British Colonies overseas and the Empire of India, and His Majesty the King of Hejaz, Najd and its Dependencies,
>
> Desiring to consolidate and strengthen the friendly relations between them and to secure and promote the interests of both nations,
>
> Are determined to conclude this Treaty of Friendship and Understanding:
>
> *Article I*
>
> His Majesty the King of Great Britain recognizes the absolute and complete independence of the territories under His Majesty the King of Hejaz, Najd and its Dependencies.[44]
>
> *Article II*
>
> Peace and friendship shall prevail between His Majesty the King of Britain and His Majesty the King of Hejaz, Najd and its Dependencies.
>
> ....
>
> *Article V*
>
> His Majesty the King of Britain shall recognize the Hejazi or Najdi nationality of all the subjects of the King of Hejaz, Najd and its

Dependencies when these are in the territories of His Majesty the King of Britain or in countries under his protection. His Majesty the King of Hejaz, Najd and its Dependencies shall also recognize the British nationality of all the subjects of His Majesty the King of Britain and of all those who enjoy his protection when these are in the territories of His Majesty the King of Hejaz, Najd and its Dependencies.

Article VI
His Majesty the King of Hejaz, Najd and its Dependencies undertakes to maintain peaceful and friendly relations with Kuwait, Bahrain and the Sheikhdoms of Qatar and the Omani coast which have special treaties with His Majesty the King of Britain.

....

Article IX
The treaty concluded between His Majesty the King of Britain and His Majesty the King of Hejaz, Najd and its Dependencies on 26 December 1915, when the King was then ruler of Najd and its Dependencies, is considered null and void as of the date of ratification of this treaty.[45]

In September 1927 the Director of Foreign Affairs of the Kingdom of Hejaz, Najd and its Dependencies, Abdullah al-Damluji, exchanged diplomatic credentials with H. Bird, the British Consul in Jiddah.

On 19 May 1927 Clayton wrote as follows to the King of Hejaz, Najd and its Dependencies:

Your Majesty,

With reference to Your Majesty's suggestion to include in the treaty an article which stipulates that His Majesty the King of Britain does not object to the procurement and import of all kinds of arms, military equipment, ammunition, machinery and other military provisions which the government of Hijaz and Najd may need to have and use,

I have the honour to inform Your Majesty that His Majesty's government feels this is a matter which does not need to be mentioned in the treaty. His Majesty's government has therefore authorized me to inform Your Majesty that the ban on the export of military equipment to the Arabian peninsula has been lifted, and that if you feel it desirable to procure any arms, ammunition or military equipment from British factories, His Majesty's government shall not object to their export nor place obstacles in the way of Your Majesty's country importing them.[46]

Results of the Kuwait Conference

The Agricultural Settlements (hijar) *and their Consequences*

It may seem that the subject of the establishment and emergence of the *hijar* (agricultural settlements) is irrelevant to this study. However, as we shall see in the pages that follow, the topic addressed here and that of the settlements can ultimately be linked.

Imam Abdul-Aziz appreciated the nature of the society over which he came to rule and never hesitated to take the appropriate steps to remedy any shortcomings or deficiencies he encountered. During the period 1910–12, the Imam decided to settle the Ikhwan by establishing a small colony around the wells of Artawiyya. He then began to expand this, transforming the well areas into agricultural colonies where the call for unity and reform was to flourish.[47]

What was particularly noteworthy was that a young man of barely 30, without any formal schooling in social studies, should initiate such a novel attempt at transforming the bases of economic and social life in his environment. He did this in a manner that was unprecedented in his country, without any knowledge of similar projects in other parts of the world, and without the necessary funds for its administration. How could such an innovatory, wide-ranging social and economic project have been undertaken without any expert advice? What was even more unusual was that the ambitious planning for such a cultural reconstruction project was undertaken when the Imam was fighting battles, and waging wars of reclamation and liberation aimed at reviving a new spirit that would replace that of tribal and individual loyalty handed down from generation to generation.[48]

Imam Abdul-Aziz had to show great firmness in dealing with the exaggerated zeal of his men, in order to extract a new element which shuns tribal fanaticism, and thus merge the various tribal blocs and in the process create one homogeneous nation. Here, the Imam had to work towards settling the bedouin in established centres known as *hijar*.

To deal with the problem of settling the bedouin, particularly those living in the border areas, the authorities in the Sultanate of Najd and its Dependencies established dozens of wells. The ultimate aim was to curb the movement of the traditional tribes in the wake of the political demarcation which the Arabian peninsula was witnessing and which was inconsistent with the former migrations dictated by bedouin custom and tribal convention. These problems had to be solved, either by a close supervision of cross-border movement or by settlement.[49]

Bedouin life could be said to resemble the land itself—arid until watered by the rain which makes it green and flourishing. The same could be said of people who go through life steeped in ignorance until a man emerges to organize, guide and thus fill them with life in every aspect of their being.[50]

Bedouin life had its dangerous side in the Arabian peninsula; hence the *hijar*, which effected the change from bedouin to sedentary life. The first *hijr* (sing. of *hijar*) was established in 1912 round the wells of Artawiyya on the way between al-Zulfi and Kuwait. This was inhabited by Sa'd bin Muthib, from Banu Harb, and was then handed over to Feisal al-Dawish and his group from the Mutair.[51]

In terms of its activities, such a settlement was an agricultural village. In military terms, however, it was one of a number of military camps scattered throughout the desert. Finally, from the viewpoint of religion, a *hijr* was rather like a splendidly furnished mosque inhabited by people who called themselves Ikhwan, a name signifying the removal of all distinctions that prevent them from being brothers in the eyes of God.[52]

The settlement of the Hejazi bedouin tribes was a more urgent problem, as it was a way of curbing the looting, theft, and the exaction of what was known as *khuwa* (protection money) which were rife. The *hijar* thus represented a fundamental transformation of bedouin life. They were also an embryonic political organization.[53]

Thus, the population was demographically classified in accordance with their lifestyle, that is, whether they were town-dwellers, bedouin or people living in the *hijar*. This last group was a new class which had never existed before under such a name. Previously, they were simply bedouin—and they would have remained as such had Imam King Abdul-Aziz not appeared. These tribes were then guided to the right religion, giving up the pre-Islamic practices and tribal customs which had long characterized their behaviour. Instead, they began to adhere to the basic principles of religion and abandoned the bedouin mode of existence, moving into a life of stability and tranquillity. The inhabitants of the *hijar* came to be known as *muhajirūn* (those who emigrate), a name which testifies to their abandoning ignorance and falsehood, in their eagerness to learn more about their new creed.[54]

With the growth of the Saudi state at the hands of King Abdul-Aziz, it became apparent that the role of the tribe had almost disappeared. In the modern state, the concept of tribe would be meaningless, as loyalty would first and foremost be owed to the state, whose institutions were bound to absorb the tribe as an individual entity.[55]

The armies which were to regain Hejaz were mostly made up of battalions from the *hijar*. These came from tribes such as the 'Utaiba, Qahtān, Subay', Hol, Banu Harb, 'Anza, Shammar, Mutair, Dhufair, 'Ajman, Banu Khalid, Banu Hajir, al-Murra, al-Dawasir, Haitham and al-'Awazim. What was the significance of this extremely important historical development? It meant that Imam Sultan Abdul-Aziz was annexing Hejaz with armies that represented not one single tribe, but the entire Arabian peninsula, or, to put it differently, the entire Sultanate of Najd and its Dependencies. Such unity is the most important characteristic of the modern state.

But no sooner had the Hejaz war ended, with the people of the *hijar* returning to their lands and villages, and with the era of stability about to commence, than what came to be known as 'the al-Dawish mutiny' began.[56] Feisal bin Sultan bin Feisal bin al-Doshan al-Dawish was one of the most important leaders of the Mutair, a grouping of various affiliated Qahtani and Adnani tribes which formed an alliance projecting a united front that extended from west of al-Ihsā' to the plains of Dabdaba or al-Daw, and then to al-Qasīm and around al-Madīnah. They discovered the error of their ways when the Imam dealt them a severe blow at the battle of Jawwalbin.

Feisal al-Dawish was the first to respond to the call for the establishment of the *hijjar*. His tribe, settled around Artawiyya, did superbly well in the Hejaz war. However, it was not long before they relapsed into their old habits and merely replaced the crudeness of their bedouin life with that of resisting all reform.

The Saudi forces which advanced toward and surrounded al-Madīnah were led by Feisal al-Dawish himself. Imam Sultan Abdul-Aziz was lenient in his treatment of others as part of his tactics during the Hejaz war, but al-Dawish failed to appreciate this and could not comprehend that a siege was not a licence for all kinds of behaviour. When he seized the village of al-'Awāli near al-Madīnah, he was dismissed by the Imam. Feisal al-Dawish returned to Artawiyya vowing revenge.[57]

Al-Dawish was uncomfortable with the civilization of Hejaz and the refined behaviour of its people. He was also loath to accept the Sultan's welcoming of innovations such as the telephone and the radio. He was unhappy with the progress of construction and angry at the treaties being signed with Europeans.[58] The ringleaders of the unrest met to plot: Feisal al-Dawish, Thaidan Hithlain (the Sheikh of the 'Ajman in the east) and Sultan bin Bijad (the Sheikh of the 'Utaiba in the west) claimed that there had been a marked change in the Imam's behaviour and that these deviations must be resisted.

When Iraq established a checkpoint at the well of Basya, which was in Iraq but on the Najdi border, this act contravened the agreements with Najd which stipulated that the wells situated on the border could not be used for military purposes. Before friendly negotiations could resume, the conspirators, led by Feisal al-Dawish, seized the opportunity to raid the checkpoint, killing all the soldiers and labourers based there. British planes pursued them, violating Najd's airspace and bombing the *hijr* of Lassaqa.

This was in contravention of Article VI of the above-mentioned Bahra agreement. The situation was critical. What would happen if Imam King Abdul-Aziz were to strike at these rebels and they sought refuge in Iraq?

The King called for a meeting of the General Assembly in Riyadh in October 1928, at which he outlined the situation. After the meeting, he went to al-Sibilla.[59] The rebels were punished. When he returned to Hejaz, however, the rebels had resumed their activities. It is here that we may note a significant historical development in the King's concern that a body of public opinion was forming which, after reliance on God alone, would be the sole basis of the youthful state developing under his guidance.[60]

The situation became even more critical when it was reported that Iraqi cars were roaming freely in the northern territories of Najd and that, while pursuing the ringleaders of the unrest, British planes were bombing peaceful civilians in Labna and other nearby Najdi lands. Faced with these developments, the King announced to the people of Najd that he had renounced their oath of allegiance and that they should elect someone else to take charge of their affairs. The whole of Najd was in uproar; people flooded into Riyadh, where a historic conference was convened and the oath of allegiance to the King renewed.[61]

The King ordered the military leaders from the ‘Utaiba, Qahtān, Banu Harb and the rest of the tribes to assemble their solders in al-Sha‘ra,[62] a village between Riyadh and Mecca in the centre of upper Najd. He rode on horseback from Riyadh to al-Sha‘ra to address them. In his speech he said:

> I have come to hear your views on the measures taken. From now on, we do not want to see in our country incidents like that which took place, nor do we want to see further satanic tendencies. Let every one of you return to his people with the good news of what you see, then come to me tomorrow to this place to declare your views openly. God willing, I shall not leave this place with the mind of any of you still corrupted by the desire to return to this unrest.

In conclusion, the entire assembly resolved that whoever had taken part in the unrest and was still alive should be stripped of all his funds, soldiers, horses and arms. The Law of Islam should decide his fate. Any *hijr* proven to be corrupt should have its members expelled, scattered among the other tribes, and denied the right to free assembly in one place. Military detachments would be sent to implement these resolutions immediately while the King was still in al-Sha‘ra.[63]

Al-Dawish fled to Iraq and contacted the British Administrative Inspector for the southern area of Iraq, Glubb Pasha, requesting asylum. King Abdul-

Aziz wrote to the British High Commissioner for Iraq on 27 December 1926, protesting at the granting of refuge to the rebels. He then travelled north and camped at Shu'aib al-Batin, 7 kilometres from the Iraqi border. When he contacted the High Commissioner, he reminded him of all the British government's previous undertakings. In response, Britain's chief accredited Representative in the Gulf requested a meeting with the King at Bunyat 'Aidan on the Iraqi border. Imam Abdul-Aziz acceded to the request and the meeting took place.

A telegram arrived from the High Commissioner confirming that Feisal al-Dawish, Naif bin Hathleen and Jasir bin Lami were all under arrest aboard a British battleship. They were later handed over. The rest of the 'Ajman and Mutair who had been expelled flooded in and gathered on the Najd border. They were immediately distributed among the various *hijar*.[64]

As for the acts of intrigue committed by Ibn Rafada, the story is as follows. He was one of the chiefs of the Bala tribe, which had settled in the northern part of Hejaz. After the annexation of Hejaz, Ibn Rafada escaped to Egypt in 1928. He was a frequent visitor to Amman and declared a rebellion in the north of Hejaz. He then headed for Egypt, passing through Aqaba, and settled in al-Shuraih. But he was opposed by the Shammar and 'Anza tribes of the northern settlements and was finally killed in the battle of Jabal Sharr near Daba.[65]

Thus, the *hijar* played an important historical role in the developments that followed the Kuwait Conference. They were supportive of Najdi authority, with which they acted in concert. The final annexation of Hejaz, the establishment of the Najdi–Hejazi Kingdom and the conclusion of treaties subsequently constituted important factors in extinguishing the unrest sparked off by one of the *hijar*.

King Abdul-Aziz was in this way able to curb his over-zealous army generals and control their violent impulses stemming from excessive tribal feeling. This enabled the King to protect Mecca and al-Madināh from the evils of extremism and excess, and to protect the people of Jiddah, including the diplomatic and consular missions and the foreign communities living there.[66]

The King did not, however, overlook the problems of the Hejaz bedouin, and the raids and the extortion of protection money to which they had been accustomed, a problem with which the Ottoman Empire could never get to grips. He called the chiefs of the various tribes and explained the dangers of raids and protection money and why he had banned them, stating that taxes were to be imposed only by the state, which was to be solely responsible for punishing offenders. The government was also active in establishing *hijar* for Hejazi tribes, determining the dues which pilgrims had to pay and warning the various tribes against making encampments on main roads. This is how King Abdul-Aziz managed to deal with the variations in social life which existed between Najd and Hejaz: the Hejazis are coast-dwellers and were therefore more exposed to the outside world, with which they had always maintained contact.[67]

The King stressed the following principles on every occasion:

- Those matters related to religion, such as religio-legal decrees, what is permissible, what is not permissible, enjoining and forbidding, are to be adjudicated by the *ulema* alone.
- Measures are to be taken by order of the governors, who act in accordance with the Shari'a.
- Individuals and groups are to refrain from settling any religious or secular issue unless resort is made to the sovereign power.
- Obligations are to be honoured.

The Kingdom of Saudi Arabia

The way the King was running the affairs of state, moving the country from the old ways to modernity and from nomadism to sedentariness, in accordance with the Shari'a, became the object of much discussion and something which impressed and was admired by everyone.

Among the consequences of the Kuwait Conference was the meeting between King Abdul-Aziz and King Feisal of Iraq aboard the British battleship HMS *Lupin* in 1930. This took place in the Arabian Gulf, which was chosen for its neutrality. The meeting was attended by the Prime Minister of Iraq, Naji al-Suwaidi, and the British High Commissioner for Iraq, Sir Francis Humphrys, who had taken over from Clayton. It resulted in an exchange of diplomatic representatives. King Feisal cabled King Abdul-Aziz, recognizing him as King of Hejaz, Najd and its Dependencies.[68]

Another treaty which linked the Kingdom with the outside world was that concluded on 10 November 1931 between the government of Hejaz, Najd and its Dependencies and the French government acting on behalf of Syria and Lebanon. The treaty was in four parts: general provisions, provisions relating to clans, provisions relating to trade, and specific provisions. In this treaty, the King of Italy recognized Imam Abdul-Aziz as King of Hejaz, Najd and its Dependencies.[69]

It was by the grace of Almighty God that the nation regained all its territories, established the modern state and strengthened the belief in the religion of God. However, the country had to be unified to become one state, with the Arabian peninsula once again becoming the cornerstone of pan-Arabism and Islam, the focal point for all Arabs and all Muslims. The unification of the Kingdom was undertaken as the means of establishing the only foundation of Arab and Islamic unity. This state is one nation, in total agreement regarding its religion, customs, conventions and aims. Thus the name of the state should not be the cause of any division. The system of government is a monarchy run in accordance with the Shari'a. This nation is an Arab nation through and through. It has its own history, and its language is that in which the Qur'ān was revealed. It is thus an Arab land, making it incumbent on its citizens to see it progress and unify in freedom and under a strong religion. The history of the Al Saud is one of sincerity, unity, pan-Arabism and Islam in the modern age. Hence the all-encompassing name: the Kingdom of Saudi Arabia, declared on 22 December 1923.

Building on this basic set of principles, the Saudi Arabian sovereign paid particular attention to the Kingdom's armed forces. Since the people of the Arabian peninsula had never been accustomed to military discipline or dress, a Ministry of Defence was established in 1946. Emir Mansour bin Abdul-Aziz was granted the rank of Lieutenant-General and was appointed the first Minister of Defence. A military revival began, and Emir Mansour donned military dress to make it popular with others. His name thus became synonymous with the renaissance of the Saudi Arabian army. He began to send missions for training in Egypt, Europe and North America, and to procure the latest military equipment. He established military academies and was particularly interested in meteorology, equipment maintenance and communications, as well as all matters relating to aviation. The Defence Ministry began to have its own annual budget. It was at the hands of Mansour bin Abdul-Aziz, then, that the Saudi Arabian army was to flourish and reach a par with other modern armies.

Thus, in terms of its various developments and consequences, the Kuwait Conference opened many doors. It was a cause with a particular effect. This, as we have seen, was the reason behind the sudden spate of progress in all fields which was to culminate in the establishment of the Kingdom of Saudi Arabia.

Though a mere drop in the ocean, it is hoped that this book has succeeded in shedding light on one aspect of a life whose hallmarks have been courage, genius, heroism, intelligence and belief in God—that of Abdul-Aziz bin Abdul Rahman al-Feisal al-Saud, who was able by the grace of God to liberate the lands of the Arabian peninsula, to achieve unity among these scattered areas within the bounds of the Shari'a, and to create a modern state whose constitution is the Qur'ān. Although these attempts were constantly thwarted by the Ottoman Empire and some of its autocratic rulers, and despite numerous internal conflicts, the third round, in the hands of Imam King Abdul-Aziz, was blessed by God.

In this way, the Arabian peninsula regained its independence and unity. Once again it came to be an Arab and Islamic power to be reckoned with and thus began to relive the days of the Wise Caliphs. It was no longer dependent on other states, as it had been from the end of the Islamic Caliphate up to the emergence of the Al Saud.

Although this book covers only a small part of the life of Imam Abdul-Aziz, it deals with an important aspect of the history of a man who created the modern Arab and Islamic history of the Arabian peninsula—Abdul-Aziz bin Abdul Rahman al-Feisal al-Saud.

Notes

Chapter 1

1. Hamad al-Jasir, *Madinat al-Riyadh 'abra Atwar al-Tarikh* (Riyadh: Dar al-Yamama, AH 1386), p. 92.
2. Husayn Khalaf Khaz'al, *Tarikh al-Jazira al-'Arabiyya fi 'Asr al-Shaykh Muhammad b. 'Abd al-Wahhab* (Beirut: Dar al-Kitab al-Lubnani, 1982), p. 238.
3. Salah al-Din al-Mukhtar, *Tarikh al-Mamlaka al-'Arabiyya al-Sa'udiyya* (Beirut: Dar Maktabat al-Hayah, 1982), vol. 2, p. 36.
4. *Madinat al-Riyadh*, p. 112.
5. Salah al-Din, *Tarikh al-Mamlaka*, vol. 2, pp. 27–33.
6. *Al-Atlas al-Tarikhi li'l-Dawla al-Sa'udiyya* (no pl.: Darat al-Malik 'Abd al-'Aziz, 1972), p. 134.
7. Muhammad Ahmad al-Badiwi, *Al-Mutawakkil 'ala al-Wudud 'Abd al-'Aziz al-Sa'ud* (Riyadh: no pub., 1977), pp. 81–6.
8. *Al-Atlas al-Tarikhi*, p. 139.
9. Salah al-Din, *Tarikh al-Mamlaka*, vol. 2, pp. 44–7.
10. *Al-Mutawakkil*, p. 108.
11. Mohammed Almana, *Arabia Unified. A Portrait of Ibn Saud* (London: Hutchinson, 1980), p. 46.
12. Salah al-Din, *Tarikh al-Mamlaka*, vol. 2, p. 83.
13. *Tarikh al-Jazira al-'Arabiyya*, p. 254.
14. Khayr al-Din al-Zirikli, *Shibh al-Jazira fi 'Ahd al-Malik 'Abd al-'Aziz* (Beirut: Dar al-'Ilm li'l-Malayin, 1977), vol. 1, p. 202.
15. Al-Hufūf.
16. 'Abd al-Fattah Abu 'Aliya, *Dirasa fi Masadir Tarikh al-Jazira al-'Arabiyya* (Riyadh: Dar al-Marikh, 1979), p. 201.
17. *Dirasa fi Masadir*, p. 199.
18. Ibid., p. 2; Salah al-Din, *Tarikh al-Mamlaka*, vol. 2, pp. 132, 157.
19. Madiha Darwish, *Tarikh al-Dawla al-Sa'udiyya* (Jiddah: Dar al-Shuruq, 1980), p. 76.
20. *Shibh al-Jazira*, vol. 1, p. 209.
21. Ibrahim 'Abd al-Rahman, *Aswad Al Sa'ud* (Beirut: Dar al-Najah, 1972), p. 137.
22. *Al-Mutawakkil*, p. 143.

23. Sayyid Ibrahim, *Tarikh al-Mamlaka al-'Arabiyya al-Sa'udiyya* (Riyadh: Maktabat al-Riyadh al-Hadith, 1973), p. 190.

24. Salah al-Din, *Tarikh al-Mamlaka*, vol. 2, p. 141.

25. Mustafa Kamal Fayid, *Tarjimat al-Dhikra al-'Arabiyya al-Dhahabiyya*, p. 51.

26. 'Abbas Mahmud al-'Aqqad, *Ma'a 'Ahil al-Jazira al-'Arabiyya* (Beirut: al-Maktaba al-'Asriyya, n.d.), p. 32.

27. *Dirasa fi Masadir*, pp. 259–63.

28. Banu Amishan, *'Abd al-'Aziz Al Sa'ud*, trans. 'Abd al-Fattah Yasin (Beirut: Dar al-Kitab al-'Arabi, n.d.), p. 110.

29. The meeting was in al-'Uqair at the end of 1915. Some sources describe Cox as the leading diplomat in the British campaign in Iraq, while others describe him as the British Representative in the Gulf.

30. Salah al-Din, *Tarikh al-Mamlaka*, vol. 2, pp. 162–70.

31. *Arabia Unified*, p. 65.

32. It is also called the treaty of Darin, which is an island opposite al-Qatīf.

33. 'Abd Allah b. Khamis, *Al-Majaz bayna al-Yamama wa al-Hijaz* (Riyadh: Dar al-Yamama, 1970), p. 66.

34. Amin Sa'id, *Tarikh al-Dawla al-Sa'udiyya* (Beirut: Dar al-Kitab al-'Arabi), vol. 1, pp. 103–5.

35. *Shibh al-Jazira*, vol. 2, p. 284; Gary Troeller, *The Birth of Saudi Arabia* (London: no pub., 1916), p. 44.

36. *Shibh al-Jazira*, vol. 3.

37. *Tarikh al-Jazira al-'Arabiyya*, pp. 291–8.

38. *Al-Mutawakkil*, p. 214.

39. *Tarikh al-Dawla*, p. 184; 'Abd al-Fattah Abu 'Aliya, *Al-Dawla al-Sa'udiyya al-Thaniya* (no pl.: Mu'assasat al-Anwar, 1977), p. 241.

40. *Dirasa fi Masadir*, pp. 259–63.

41. Salah al-Din, *Tarikh al-Mamlaka*, vol. 2, pp. 220–4.

42. *Tarjimat al-Dhikra*, p. 51.

43. *Al-Mutawakkil*, p. 161.

44. Wizarat al-Kharijiyya, *Al-Kitab al-Akhdar al-Najdi*, pp. 55–9.

45. Lady Anne Blunt, *A Pilgrimage to Nejd* (London: John Murray, 1881. Reprint: London, Darf, 1984).

46. Salah al-Din, *Tarikh al-Mamlaka*, vol. 2, p. 241.

47. *Shibh al-Jazira*, vol. 2, p. 531.

48. *Al-Mutawakkil*, p. 149.

49. Ahmad 'Abd al-Ghafur 'Attar, *Saqr al-Jazira* (Jiddah: Matabi' al-Mu'assasa al-'Arabiyya, AH 1384), vol. 2, p. 246.

50. *Saqr al-Jazira*, vol. 2, pp. 246–7.

51. *Shibh al-Jazira*, vol. 2, p. 246.

52. ‘Umar al-Faruq Rajab, *Dirasat fi Jughrafiyat al-Mamlaka al-‘Arabiyya al-Sa‘udiyya* (Jiddah: Dar al-Shuruq, 1978), pp. 68–141.

53. *Aswad Al Sa‘ud*, p. 144; *Tarikh al-Jazira al-‘Arabiyya*, p. 300; Fu’ad Hamza, *Qalb Jazirat al-‘Arab* (Riyadh: Maktabat al-Nasr al-Haditha, 1968), p. 147.

54. Munir al-‘Ajlani, *Tarikh al-Bilad al-‘Arabiyya al-Sa‘udiyya* (Beirut: Dar al-Kitab al-‘Arabi), vol. 4, p. 378.

55. Salah al-Din, *Tarikh al-Mamlaka*, vol. 2, pp. 243–376, 379.

56. See note 45 above for publishing details.

57. ‘Abd Allah al-‘Ali al-Zamil, *Asdaq al-Bunud fi Tarikh ‘Abd al-‘Aziz Al Sa‘ud* (Beirut: al-Mu’assasa al-Tijariyya, 1972), p. 259.

58. Salah al-Din, *Tarikh al-Mamlaka*, vol. 2, pp. 92, 166.

59. *Al-Mutawakkil*, p. 145.

60. Raja’ al-Khattab, *Al-‘Iraq min 1921–1927* (Najaf: Matba‘t al-Nu‘man, 1976), p. 294.

61. Sayf al-Shamlan, *Min Tarikh al-Kuwayt* (Cairo: Matba‘t Nahdat Misr, 1959), p. 150.

62. *Asdaq al-Bunud*, p. 367.

63. *Qalb Jazirat al-‘Arab*, p. 386.

64. *Tarikh al-Bilad*, pp. 375, 376. Based on *Lam‘ al-Shihab fi Sirat Muhammad b. ‘Abd al-Wahhab*, by either an unknown writer or Hasan al-Rabki.

65. ‘Abd al-Razzaq al-Daraji, *Ja‘far Abu’l-Thaman* (Baghdad: Dar al-Rashid, n.d.), pp. 150–4.

66. *Qalb Jazirat al-‘Arab*, p. 386.

67. ‘Umar al-Faruq Rajab, *Al-Hijaz* (Beirut: Dar al-Shuruq, 1979), pp. 307–8.

68. *Al-Majaz*, p. 60.

69. *Shibh al-Jazira*, vol. 2, p. 263; *Asdaq al-Bunud*, p. 130; *Arabia Unified*, pp. 78, 80.

Chapter 2

1. Albert Lybyer, *The Turkish Parliament*, p. 101.

2. Hassan ‘Ali Hallaq, *Mawqif al-Dawla al-‘Uthmaniyya min al-Haraka al-Sahiyuniyya* (Beirut: no pub., 1978), pp. 230–3; Zayn al-Zayn, *Nushu’ al-Qawmiyya al-‘Arabiyya* (Beirut: no pub., 1968), pp. 85–90.

3. ‘Abd al-Karim Rafiq, *Al-‘Arab wa al-‘Uthmaniyyun* (Damascus: Maktabat Atlas, 1974), pp. 535–45.

4. Hasan Sabri al-Khawli, *Siyasat al-Isti'màr al-Sahiyuniyya* (Cairo: Dar al-Ma'arif, 1973), pp. 120–1.

5. Carl Brockelmann (ed.), *History of the Islamic People* (London: Routledge & Kegan Paul, 1948).

6. Ahmad Qadri, *Mudhakkirati 'an al-Thawra al-'Arabiyya al-Kubra* (Damascus: no pub., 1956), pp. 10, 15.

7. Khayriyya Qasimiyya, *Al-Hukuma al-'Arabiyya fi Dimashq* (Cairo: Dar al-Ma'arif, 1971), p. 26.

8. 'Abd al-Karim Rafiq, *Al-'Arab wa'l-'Uthmaniyyun* (Damascus: Maktabat Atlas, 1974), pp. 475, 476.

9. This was a British office established during the First World War to further British policy. It used to be attached to the office of the High Commissioner in Cairo.

10. Salah al-Din al-Mukhtar, *Tarikh al-Mamlaka al-'Arabiyya al-Sa'udiyya* (Beirut: Dar Maktabat al-Hayah, 1982), vol. 2, p. 171.

11. *Al-Hukuma al-'Arabiyya*, pp. 26, 27. Ronald Storrs was the author of *Orientations* (London: Ivor Nicholson & Watson, 1937).

12. Khayr al-Din al-Zirikli, *Shibh al-Jazira fi 'Ahd al-Malik 'Abd al-'Aziz* (Beirut: Dar al-'Ilm li'l-Malayin, 1977), vol. 1, pp. 215, 216.

13. Al-Sayyid Salim, *Takwin al-Yaman al-Hadith* (Cairo: Maktabat Sa'id Ra'fat, 1971), pp. 221, 222.

14. *Al-Hukuma al-'Arabiyya*, p. 27.

15. He served as Secretary of State for War in Asquith's cabinet.

16. *Tarikh al-Mamlaka*, vol. 2, p. 160.

17. *Siyasat al-Isti'mar*, p. 136.

18. *Al-Hukuma al-'Arabiyya*, p. 28.

19. *Tarikh al-Shu'ub*, pp. 744, 745.

20. *Tarikh al-Mamlaka*, vol. 2, p. 178.

21. In his third letter, Hussein relinquished the *vilayet* of Mersin. In his fourth letter he relinquished Jabal Lubnan and left Iraq to what he called the justice and wisdom of Britain.

22. *Siyasat al-Isti'mar*, p. 37.

23. *Al-Hukuma al-'Arabiyya*, p. 174; *Tarikh al-Shu'ub*, pp. 745, 774.

24. *Al-Hukuma al-'Arabiyya*, pp. 37, 38.

25. *Siyasat al-Isti'mar*, p. 178.

26. The author of *The Seven Pillars of Wisdom.*

27. *Tarikh al-Shu'ub*, p. 748.

28. Ibid., p. 759.

29. Asquith's cabinet resigned in December 1916. The War Office was established under Lloyd George, Balfour entering it as Foreign Secretary.

30. *Al-Hukuma al-'Arabiyya*, p. 41.
31. *Pravda* published the whole text.
32. *Siyasat al-Isti'mar*, p. 240.
33. *Tarikh al-Shu'ub*, p. 749.
34. A town on the Italian Riviera.
35. *Siyasat al-Isti'mar*, p. 406.
36. Known as Namibia since 1968.
37. W. Ireland, *Iraq*, pp. 260–70.
38. Muhammad Awad Muhammad, *Al-Isti'mar wa'l-Madhahib al-Isti'mariyya* (Cairo: Dar al-Kitab al-'Arabi, 1956), pp. 56–9.
39. I.e. the Ottoman Empire.
40. The countries which were possessions of the Ottoman Empire were classed as 'category A'.
41. *Siyasat al-Isti'mar*, p. 407.
42. *Al-Hukuma al-'Arabiyya*, p. 175.
43. *Tarikh al-Shu'ub*, p. 749.
44. Ibid., p. 176.
45. Ahmad 'Assa, *Mu'jiza fawq al-Rimal*, pp. 77, 78.
46. This was the consequence of what was known as the uprising of al-Shām in 1860. In this, Britain had supported the Druse while France had supported the Maronites.
47. *Tarikh al-Shu'ub*, pp. 761–2.
48. *Mu'jiza*, pp. 78–9.
49. Ibid., p. 79.
50. Muhammad Khaduri, *Asbab al-Ihtilal al-Britani li'l-'Iraq* (Mosul: no pub., 1933), pp. 20–4.
51. *Tarikh al-Shu'ub*, p. 775.
52. Raja' al-Khattab, *Al-'Iraq min 1921–1927* (Najaf: Matba't al-Nu'man, 1976), p. 19.
53. *Al-'Iraq*, p. 81.
54. Ibid., pp. 179, 260.
55. *Tarikh al-Shu'ub*, pp. 772, 773.

Chapter 3

1. *Al-Atlas al-Tarikhi li'l-Dawla al-Sa'udiyya* (no pl.: Darat al-Malik 'Abd al-'Aziz, 1972), pp. 172–4.
2. Khayr al-Din al-Zirikli, *Shibh al-Jazira fi 'Ahd al-Malik 'Abd al-'Aziz* (Beirut: Dar al-'Ilm li'l-Malayin, 1977), vol. 1, p. 184.

3. 'Umar al-Faruq Rajab, *Al-Hijaz* (Beirut: Dar al-Shuruq, 1979), pp. 42–4.

4. 'Abd Allah b. Khamis, *Al-Majaz bayna al-Yamama wa al-Hijaz* (Riyadh: Dar al-Yamama, 1970), p. 328.

5. 'Atiq al-Biladi, *Mu'jam Ma'alim al-Hijaz* (Mecca: Mu'assasat Mecca, 1978), vol. 2, p. 22; vol. 3, p. 23.

6. *Al-Atlas al-Tarikhi*, p. 168; Mohammed Almana, *Arabia Unified. A Portrait of Ibn Saud* (London: Hutchinson, 1980), pp. 63, 64.

7. Ahmad Husayn, *Walid wa ma Walad* (Beirut: al-Maktaba al-'Asriyya, 1975), pp. 64, 65.

8. Muhammad Ahmad al-Badiwi, *Al-Mutawakkil 'ala al-Wudud 'Abd al-'Aziz al-Sa'ud* (Riyadh: no pub., 1977), pp. 198, 199; Fu'ad Hamza, *Qalb Jazirat al-'Arab* (Riyadh: Maktabat al-Nasr al-Haditha, 1968), p. 383.

9. *Al-Mutawakkil*, p. 184.

10. Madiha Darwish, *Tarikh al-Dawla al-Sa'udiyya* (Jiddah: Dar al-Shuruq, 1980), pp. 90–5.

11. Salah al-Din al-Mukhtar, *Tarikh al-Mamlaka al-'Arabiyya al-Sa'udiyya* (Beirut: Dar Maktabat al-Hayah, 1982), vol. 2, p. 123.

12. Mustafa Kamal Fayid, *Tarjimat al-Dhikra al-'Arabiyya al-Dhahabiyya*, p. 88.

13. *Tarikh al-Mamlaka*, vol. 2, pp. 121–2.

14. *Al-Mutawakkil*, p. 196.

15. *Al-Atlas al-Tarikhi*, pp. 166, 167.

16. *Tarikh al-Mamlaka*, vol. 2, pp. 198, 200.

17. Ahmad 'Abd al-Ghafur 'Attar, *Saqr al-Jazira* (Jiddah: Matabi' al-Mu'assasa al-'Arabiyya, AH 1384), vol. 2, p. 274.

18. Sayf al-Shamlan, *Min Tarikh al-Kuwayt* (Cairo: Matba't Nahdat Misr, 1959), pp. 185, 186.

19. 'Abd Allah al-'Ali al-Zamil, *Asdaq al-Bunud fi Tarikh 'Abd al-'Aziz Al Sa'ud* (Beirut: al-Mu'assasa al-Tijariyya, 1972), p. 367.

20. *Shibh al-Jazira*, vol. 2, p. 486.

21. Formulated in al-'Uqair on 1 December 1922.

22. Amin al-Rihani, *Muluk al-'Arab* (Beirut: no pub., 1923), vol. 2, p. 55.

23. Wizarat al-Kharijiyya, Mecca, *Majmu'at al-Mu'ahadat* (Mecca: Matba'at Umm Qura, AH 1350), pp. 1–2.

24. *Majmu'at al-Mu'ahadat*. This treaty was signed on 5 May 1922.

25. Signed in al-'Uqair on 2 December 1922.

26. *Al-Mutawakkil*, p. 162.

27. *Asdaq al-Bunud*, pp. 258, 293, 356; *Saqr al-Jazira*, vol. 2, p. 414.

28. Banu Amishan, *'Abd al-'Aziz al-Sa'ud*, trans. 'Abd al-Fattah Yasin (Beirut: Dar al-Kitab al-'Arabi, n.d.), pp. 163–5.

29. Lady Anne Blunt, *A Pilgrimage to Nejd* (London: John Murray, 1881. Reprint: London, Darf, 1984).

30. Muhammad 'Abd al-Mun'im al-Sayyid al-Raqid, *Al-Ghazuw al-'Uthmani li Misr* (Cairo: no pub., 1972), pp. 225–30.

31. Muhammad al-Bahrawi, *Fath al-'Uthmaniyyin 'Adan*, pp. 84–7, 182.

32. *Shibh al-Jazira*, vol. 1, p. 149.

33. Amin Sa'id, *Tarikh al-Dawla al-Sa'udiyya* (Beirut: Dar al-Kitab al-'Arabi), vol. 1, p. 183.

34. Madiha Darwish, *Tarikh al-Dawla*, p. 75.

35. *Al-Atlas al-Tarikhi*, p. 136.

36. Madiha Darwish, *Tarikh al-Dawla*, p. 75.

37. *Tarikh al-Mamlaka*, vol. 2, pp. 70–80.

38. Ibid., vol. 2, pp. 85–90.

39. *Shibh al-Jazira*, vol. 1, p. 173.

40. *Tarikh al-Mamlaka*, vol. 2, pp. 159–60.

41. Khayriyya Qasimiyya, *Al-Hukuma al-'Arabiyya fi Dimashq* (Cairo: Dar al-Ma'arif, 1971), p. 23.

42. *Tarikh al-Mamlaka*, vol. 2, pp. 161, 163.

43. Ahmad 'Assa, *Mu'jiza fawq al-Rimal*.

44. 'Abd al-Karim Rafiq, *Al-'Arab wa al-'Uthmaniyyun* (Damascus: Maktabat Atlas, 1974), pp. 558–9; Gary Troeller, *The Birth of Saudi Arabia* (London: no pub., 1916), pp. 75–80.

45. Jad Taha, *Siyasat Britaniya fi Junub al-Yaman* (no pl.: Dar al-Fikr al-'Arabi, 1970), pp. 36–40, 175–80; Muhammad Isma'il al-Nadawi, *Tarikh al-Silat bayna al-Hind wa'l-Bilad al-'Arabiyya*, pp. 245, 247.

46. Sayyid Nawfal, *Al-Khalij al-'Arabi* (Beirut: Dar al-Tali'a, 1969), pp. 178, 181; Sayf al-Shamlan, *Min Tarikh al-Kuwayt* (Cairo: Matba't Nahdat Misr, 1959), p. 121.

47. *Tarikh al-Mamlaka*, vol. 2, p. 69.

48. Mustafa Kamal Fayid, *Tarjimat al-Dhikra al-'Arabiyya al-Dhahabiyya*, pp. 13, 46.

49. *Tarikh al-Mamlaka*, vol. 2, p. 173.

50. *Tarjimat al-Dhikra*, p. 52.

51. *Shibh al-Jazira*, vol. 1, p. 280.

52. *Min Tarikh al-Kuwayt*, p. 163.

53. East of al-Zulfi and north of Artawiyya; the battle in which Shakespear was killed.

54. *Qalb Jazirat al-'Arab*, pp. 380, 381.

55. The treaty of Jiddah, 20 May 1927.
56. *Tarikh al-Mamlaka*, vol. 2, pp. 175, 176.
57. Madiha Darwish, *Tarikh al-Dawla*, pp. 78, 79.
58. *Shibh al-Jazira*, vol. 1, p. 285; *Qalb Jazirat al-'Arab*, p. 381.
59. *Min Tarikh al-Kuwayt*, p. 181.
60. *Qalb Jazirat al-'Arab*, p. 381.
61. *Tarikh al-Mamlaka*, vol. 2, p. 175.
62. Ibid., vol. 2, p. 215.
63. Hafiz Wahba, *Khamsun 'Aman fi Jazirat al-'Arab* (Cairo: Maktabat wa Matba'at Mustafa al-Babi al-Halabi, 1960), p. 74.
64. The 'Uqair agreement.
65. *Al-Mutawakkil*, pp. 152–7.
66. *Tarjimat al-Dhikra*, p. 90.
67. *'Abd al-'Aziz al-Sa'ud*, p. 156.
68. *Tarjimat al-Dhikra*, p. 94.
69. *Al-Mutawakkil*, pp. 159, 176.
70. Madiha Darwish, *Tarikh al-Dawla*, p. 114.

Chapter 4

1. Madiha Darwish, *Tarikh al-Dawla al-Sa'udiyya* (Jiddah: Dar al-Shuruq, 1980), p. 101.
2. The Khorramshahr of today. Khayr al-Din al-Zirikli, *Shibh al-Jazira fi 'Ahd al-Malik 'Abd al-'Aziz* (Beirut: Dar al-'Ilm li'l-Malayin, 1977), vol. 1, p. 288.
3. 'Abd al-Fattah Abu 'Aliya, *Dirasa fi Masadir Tarikh al-Jazira al-'Arabiyya* (Riyadh: Dar al-Marikh, 1979), p. 205.
4. 'Abd Allah b. Khamis, *Al-Majaz bayna al-Yamama wa al-Hijaz* (Riyadh: Dar al-Yamama, 1970), p. 84.
5. Fu'ad Hamza, *Qalb Jazirat al-'Arab* (Riyadh: Maktabat al-Nasr al-Haditha, 1968), pp. 388, 391.
6. *Shibh al-Jazira*, vol. 1, pp. 366–70.
7. Muhammad Ahmad al-Badiwi, *Al-Mutawakkil 'ala al-Wudud 'Abd al-'Aziz al-Sa'ud* (Riyadh: no pub., 1977), p. 199.
8. *Al-Mutawakkil*, p. 202; *Shibh al-Jazira*, vol. 1, p. 325.
9. 'Abd al-Razzaq al-Daraji, *Ja'far Abu'l-Thaman* (Baghdad: Dar al-Rashid, n.d.), p. 203.
10. Regions called salt swamps containing salt deposits. Among them are the salt swamp of Quriyyat al-Milh and that of al-Haduda' in Wādī al-Sarhan.

11. Mustafa Kamal Fayid, *Tarjimat al-Dhikra al-'Arabiyya al-Dhahabiyya*, p. 104.

12. Ahmad 'Abd al-Ghafur 'Attar, *Saqr al-Jazira* (Jiddah: Matabi' al-Mu'assasa al-'Arabiyya, AH 1384), vol. 2, p. 274.

13. Mrs Hogarth is also known as Mrs Rosita Forbes.

14. Foreign Office Document 686-129, Copy 16420, Cairo, 2 April 1923.

15. Report on Southern Arabia, by Kamal Fahmi to Field Marshal Viscount Allenby, High Commissioner for Egypt, Foreign Office Document 686-129, File No. 372.

16. Wizarat al-Kharijiyya, *Al-Kitab al-Akhdar al-Najdi. Mu'tamar al-Kuwayt*, pp. 4, 5.

17. *Al-Kitab al-Akhdar*, pp. 5, 6.

18. F.O. Document 686-135 B5, No. 32, 1 November 1923, File 428.

19. F.O. Document 686-135-3117.

20. *Al-Kitab al-Akhdar*, pp. 6, 7.

21. F.O. Document 371-9996 P.3117, No. 85.

22. F.O. Document 686-135-3117, 2 November 1923.

23. F.O. Document 686-135, No. 34.

24. F.O. Document 686-135, File No. 428.

25. F.O. Document 686-135, File No. 428.

26. F.O. Document 686-135 B5.

27. F.O. Document 686-135, No. 38. A document written in Arabic, in the handwriting of King Hussein, entitled 'The British Representative in Jiddah, No. 38', and a document which has a translation entitled 'Translation No. 38'.

28. F.O. Document 686-135, No. 54, File No. 428.

29. F.O. Document 686-135 M.1923 R.T.C.3, No. 35, 18 November 1923.

30. F.O. Document 686-135 M.23 R.T.C.3, No. 36, 18 November 1923, File No. 428, Copy 11-7-1.

31. F.O. Document 371-9996, P.3117,84, 29 November 1923.

32. F.O. Document 371-9996, P.3117,83, No. 1835, Amman, 25 November 1923.

33. F.O. Document 371-9996, P.3117,86, No. 336, Amman.

34. F.O. Document 686-135, 3117 Economic Code No. T.13, 2 December 1923.

35. F.O. Document 686-135 M.23, No. 40, File No. 428.

36. F.O. Document 686-135, 3117, M.23, No. 59, File No. 428.

37. F.O. Document 686-135, No. 19, 20, File No. 428.

38. F.O. Document 686-135, 3117, No. 27, 16 December 1923, File No. 428.

39. F.O. Document 686-135, Economic Code No.118 M., File No. 428.

40. *Al-Kitab al-Akhdar*, pp. 22, 23.

41. Ibid., pp. 24–5.

42. F.O. Document 686-135, 18 December 1923.

43. F.O. Document 686-135, 18 December 1923.

44. *Al-Kitab al-Akhdar*, p. 25; F.O. Document 686-135, 3117, No. 33.

45. F.O. Document 371-9996, P.3117, No. 27 of 1923, 18 December 1923.

46. *Al-Kitab al-Akhdar*, p. 30.

47. Ibid., p. 33; F.O. Document 686-135, 3117, M.1921, No. 35, File No. 428, 22 December 1923.

48. F.O. Document 686-135, 3117, No. 144, E 11670-678-91.

49. F.O. Document 686-135, 3117, M.1921, No. 62, File No. 428.

50. *Al-Kitab al-Akhdar*, pp. 36–7.

51. F.O. Document 371-9996, P.3117, 29 December 1923.

52. F.O. Document 371-9996, P.3117, 29 December 1923.

53. An allusion to the situation during the first and second Saudi states.

54. *Al-Kitab al-Akhdar*, pp. 38–9.

55. Ibid., pp. 40–1.

56. F.O. Document 371-9996, P.3117, 28 December 1923.

57. *Al-Kitab al-Akhdar*, p. 44.

58. F.O. Document 371-9996, P.3117, 1 January 1924. Received by Colonial Office, 18 January 1924.

59. F.O. Document 371-9996, P.3117, 3 January 1924.

60. F.O. Document 371-9996, P.3117, 4 January 1924.

61. F.O. Document 371-9996, P.3117, 6 January 1924.

62. F.O. Document 371-9996, P.3117, 6 January 1924.

63. F.O. Document 371-9996, P.3117, No. 46, 6 January 1924.

64. F.O. Document 371-9996, 1078-24, 8 January 1924.

65. F.O. Document 371-9996, P.3117; extract from Intelligence Report No. 1, Baghdad, 10 January 1924; letter from the Colonial Office of 23 January 1924, Ref. No. 3670-24, E812-4-91, 3886-24.

66. Ibid.

67. F.O. Document 371-9996, P.3117, 15 January 1924.

68. F.O. Document 371-9996, P.3117 11 January 1924. Received by Colonial Office, 14 January 1924.

69. *Al-Kitab al-Akhdar*, pp. 47–8.

70. By this is indicated the instructions of Devonshire, the Secretary of State for Colonial Affairs, dated 8 January 1924, to which we have referred previously.

71. F.O. Document 686-135, 3117 M.1923, File No. 11-7-1, Copy 428,390, No. 2, 18 January 1924.

72. F.O. Document 686-135, M.1921, No. 85, File No. 428, 15 January 1924.

73. F.O. Document 686-135, M.1923, No. 2, File No. 11-7-1.

74. F.O. Document 371-9996, P.3117, No. 19, a copy to the Colonial Office; No. 30, a copy to Knox in Kuwait, 20 January 1924.

75. F.O. Document 371-9996, P.3117, Downing Street, 22 January 1924, No. 2819-24.

76. F.O. Document 371-9996, P.3117, 21 June 1924.

77. *Al-Kitab al-Akhdar*, pp. 52–5.

78. F.O. Document 686-135, 3117 M.1921, No. 31, 22 January 1924, File No. 428, Copy 11-7-1.

79. F.O. Document 686-135, to the Secretary of State for the Colonies.

80. F.O. Document 371-9996, P.3117, 26 June 1924.

81. F.O. Document 371-9996, P.3117.

82. *Al-Kitab al-Akhdar*, pp. 59, 60.

83. F.O. Document 686-135, 3111 E.1622-4-91, 6681-24, P.C. 6209-24. The document is a letter from the Colonial Office dated 9 February 1924. One copy was sent to the Air Ministry and another to the Government of India.

84. As above.

85. *Al-Kitab al-Akhdar*, pp. 65–7.

86. ‘Abd Allah b. Khamis, *Al-Majaz bayna al-Yamama wa al-Hijaz* (Riyadh: Dar al-Yamama, 1970), p. 84; Khalid al-Faraj, *Ahsan al-Qisas* (Cairo: Dar al-Ma‘arif, 1971), p. 119.

87. Sheikh Hafiz Wahba, *Arabian Days* (London: Arthur Barker, 1964), p. 146.

Chapter 5

1. Mustafa Kamal Fayid, *Tarjimat al-Dhikra al-‘Arabiyya al-Dhahabiyya*, p. 106.

2. Sayyid Ibrahim, *Tarikh al-Mamlaka al-‘Arabiyya al-Sa‘udiyya* (Riyadh: Maktabat al-Riyadh al-Hadith, 1973), vol. 2, p. 268.

3. Muhammad Isma‘il al-Nadawi, *Tarikh al-Silat bayna al-Hind wa’l-Bilad al-‘Arabiyya*, p. 146.

4. 'Uthman b. Bashr, *'Unwan al-Majd fi Tarikh Najd* (Riyadh: Matabi' al-Qasim, AH 1385), pp. 103–73.

5. Madiha Darwish, *Tarikh al-Dawla al-Sa'udiyya* (Jiddah: Dar al-Shuruq, 1980), p. 104.

6. *Tarikh al-Mamlaka*, vol. 2, p. 291.

7. Muhammad Ahmad al-Badiwi, *Al-Mutawakkil 'ala al-Wudud 'Abd al-'Aziz al-Sa'ud* (Riyadh: no pub., 1977), pp. 214–28.

8. *Al-Mutawakkil*, p. 223.

9. Hafiz Wahba, *Khamsun 'Aman fi Jazirat al-'Arab* (Cairo: Maktabat wa Matba'at Mustafa al-Babi al-Halabi, 1960), p. 57.

10. *Umm Qura*, Nos. 1–5, Jamadi al-Awwal AH 1343.

11. *Tarikh al-Mamlaka*, vol. 2, p. 380.

12. Ahmad 'Abd al-Ghafur 'Attar, *Saqr al-Jazira* (Jiddah: Matabi' al-Mu'assasa al-'Arabiyya, AH 1384), vol. 2, p. 398.

13. *Al-Mutawakkil*, p. 237.

14. A prosperous town halfway between Mecca and Jiddah. When Ibn Jubayr passed by it in AH 570 it was known as al-Qarin. Today, Qarin is the name of the small hill on the eastern side of the town. The town became known as Bahra (i.e. 'pool') because a well was dug which never runs dry.

15. Wizarat al-Kharijiyya, Mecca, *Majmu'at al-Mu'ahadat* (Mecca: Matba'at Umm Qura, AH 1350).

16. *Majmu'at al-Mu'ahadat*, pp. 11, 12, 13. This agreement was signed in an encampment in Bahra on 1 November 1925.

17. Ibid., pp. 14, 15.

18. Ibid., pp. 15, 16. It was signed in Jiddah on 2 November 1925.

19. Ibid., pp. 17, 18.

20. *Khamsun 'Aman*, pp. 83, 85.

21. *Saqr al-Jazira*, vol. 2, p. 315.

22. *Tarjimat al-Dhikra*, p. 4.

23. *Tarikh al-Dawla*, p. 124.

24. *Umm Qura*, 22 Jamadi al-Awwal AH 1343.

25. *Tarikh al-Mamlaka*, vol. 2, pp. 384–7.

26. 'Abd Allah al-'Ali al-Zamil, *Asdaq al-Bunud fi Tarikh 'Abd al-'Aziz al-Sa'ud* (Beirut: al-Mu'assasa al-Tijariyya, 1972), pp. 199–203.

27. *Umm Qura*, 22 Jamadi al-Awwal AH 1343.

28. *Asdaq al-Bunud*, p. 238. 'Public Prosecutor' was the title of Prince Feisal in the Hejaz when King Abdul-Aziz was in Najd.

29. *Majmu'at al-Mu'ahadat*, pp. 19–21. It was signed on 19 March 1926.

30. Al-Sayyid Salim, *Takwin al-Yaman al-Hadith* (Cairo: Maktabat Sa'id Ra'fat, 1971), p. 170.

31. *Tarikh al-Mamlaka*, vol. 2, pp. 262, 263.

32. Ibid., vol. 2, p. 393.

33. *Khamsun 'Aman*, p. 78.

34. 'Abd Allah b. Khamis, *Al-Majaz bayna al-Yamama wa al-Hijaz* (Riyadh: Dar al-Yamama, 1970), p. 120.

35. *Khamsun 'Aman*, p. 78.

36. Khayr al-Din al-Zirikli, *Shibh al-Jazira fi 'Ahd al-Malik 'Abd al-'Aziz* (Beirut: Dar al-'Ilm li'l-Malayin, 1977), vol. 1, p. 381.

37. *Shibh al-Jazira*, vol. 1, pp. 402–13.

38. Madiha Darwish, 'Al-'Alaqat al-Sa'udiyya al-Misriyya 1924–1936', unpub. PhD dissertation, 1978, pp. 252–67.

39. *Majmu'at al-Mu'ahadat*, pp. 23, 24. It was signed on 21 October 1926.

40. *Al-Mutawakkil*, p. 245.

41. *Tarikh al-Dawla*, p. 128.

42. *Shibh al-Jazira*, vol. 2, p. 427.

43. *Khamsun 'Aman*, p. 138.

44. *Majmu'at al-Mu'ahadat*, pp. 33, 34.

45. Ibid., pp. 34, 35. It was signed on behalf of Britain by Sir Gilbert Clayton on 20 May 1927.

46. Ibid., p. 37.

47. *Tarjimat al-Dhikra*, p. 56.

48. *Al-Majaz*, p. 60.

49. 'Umar al-Faruq Rajab, *Dirasat fi Jughrafiyat al-Mamlaka al-'Arabiyya al-Sa'udiyya* (Jiddah: Dar al-Shuruq, 1978), p. 149.

50. Khayr al-Din Zirikli, *Al-Wajiz fi Sirat al-Malik 'Abd al-'Aziz* (Beirut: Dar al-'Ilm li'l-Malayin, 1972), p. 251.

51. *Shibh al-Jazira*, vol. 1, p. 263.

52. Fu'ad Hamza, *Qalb Jazirat al-'Arab* (Riyadh: Maktabat al-Nasr al-Haditha, 1968), p. 30.

53. Carl Brockelmann (ed.), *History of the Islamic People* (London, Routledge & Kegan Paul, 1948); Mohammed Almana, *Arabia Unified. A Portrait of Ibn Saud* (London: Hutchinson, 1980), p. 81.

54. *Qalb Jazirat al-'Arab*, p. 101.

55. 'Umar al-Faruq Rajab, *Al-Hijaz* (Beirut: Dar al-Shuruq, 1979), pp. 307, 308.

56. *Al-Wajiz*, p. 109.

57. *Tarikh al-Mamlaka*, vol. 2, pp. 382, 383.

58. *Saqr al-Jazira*, vol. 2, p. 414.
59. Rawdat al-Sibilla.
60. *Asdaq al-Bunud*, p. 280.
61. *Al-Mutawakkil*, p. 164.
62. 1 Jamada al-Awwal 1348/1929.
63. *Asdaq al-Bunud*, p. 244.
64. *Shibh al-Jazira*, vol. 2, p. 504.
65. *Al-Wajiz*, p. 156.
66. *Al-Majaz*, p. 102.
67. *Asdaq al-Bunud*, p. 287.
68. *Shibh al-Jazira*, vol. 2, p. 370.
69. *Majmu'at al-Mu'ahadat*, pp. 121–5.

Bibliography

DOCUMENTS AND PERIODICALS

Umm Qura. No. 1, 5 Jamada al-Ula, AH 1343.

———No. 91, 3 Rabi' al-Awwal, AH 1345.

Wizarat al-Kharijiyya. Mecca. *Majmu'at al-Mu'ahadat. 1341/1922–1350/1931*. Mecca: Matba'at Umm Qura, AH 1350.

———*Al-Kitab al-Akhdar. Mu'tamar Kuwayt*.

Foreign Office Documents

686–129. File No. 372. Report on Southern Arabia, by Kamal Fahmi to Field Marshal Viscount Allenby, High Commissioner for Egypt.

686–135. M.1921. No. 57. British Agent to Foreign Office, 25 Nov. 1923.

686–135 3117. Economic Code No. T.13. Trevor, Bushire, to British Agent, 2 Dec. 1923.

686–135. M.23. No. 40. Foreign Office to British Agent, 7 Dec. 1923.

686–135 3117. M.23. No. 59. British Agent to Foreign Office, 8 Dec. 1923.

686–135 3117. M.1921. No. 20. Knox, Kuwait, to British Agent, 8 Dec. 1923.

686–135 3117. M.1921. No. 23. File No. 428. Copy 70. Knox, Kuwait, to British Agent, 10 Dec. 1923.

686–135 3117. Economic Code No. 118m. British Agent, Jiddah, to Knox, Kuwait, 17 Dec. 1923.

686–135 3117. M.1921. No. 29. Knox, Kuwait, to British Agent, Jiddah, 17 Dec. 1923.

686–135 3117. No. 31. Knox, Kuwait, to Colonial Office, London, 18 Dec. 1923, and No. 32, 21 Dec. 1923.

686–135 3117. Economic Code. Political Resident, Bushire, to British Agent, Jiddah, 18 Dec. 1923.

686–135 3117. No. 159–S. Confidential. Political Agent, Kuwait, HBMS Consul, Jiddah, Kuwait Conference.

686–135 3117. No. 61. File No. 428. British Agent, Jiddah, to Trevor, Bushire, 19 Dec. 1923.

686–135 3117. Telegram No. 32. Knox to Colonial Office, 21 Dec. 1923.

686–135 3117. Nos 33, 34. Knox, Kuwait, to Colonial Office, Jiddah, 21 Dec. 1923.

686–135 3117. M.1921. No. 35. Knox, Kuwait, to British Agent, 22 Dec. 1923.
686–135 3117. No. 62. File No. 428. British Agent to Foreign Office, 25 Dec. 1923.
686–135 3117. M.1921. No. 31. Copy No. 11–7–1. File No. 428. High Commissioner, Jerusalem, to British Agent, Jiddah, 22 Jan. 1924.
686–135 3117. Copy E1622–4–91, 6681–24. Subject: Kuwait Conference. Interview between High Commissioner for Palestine and King Hussein at Amman on 21 Jan. 1924. Signed E.T. Richmond, 1924. [Not an invitation for King Hussein to participate in the Kuwait Conference.]
686–135 3117. Palestine. Secret. Reference No. T.J.–221. Government House, Jerusalem, 1 Feb. 1924. Signed Herbert Samuel, High Commissioner, to the Right Hon. J.H. Thomas, P.C., M.P., His Majesty's Principal Secretary of State for the Colonies.
686–135. M.1921. No. 38. Copy 428. From Foreign Office, London, to British Agent, 22 Feb. 1922.
686–135 3117. Palestine. Secret. Ref. No. T.J.–221. Government House, Jerusalem. From Herbert Samuel, High Commissioner, to the Right Hon. J.H. Thomas, P.C., M.P., His Majesty's Principal Secretary of State for the Colonies.
371–9996. P.3117. No. 1838. Translation of credentials of Col. Ali Khulqi Bey, envoy of Transjordan at Kuwait Conference 1923, 25 Nov. 1923.
371–9996. P.3117. No. 336. Translation of letter of instruction from Amir Abdullah to Col. Ali Khulqi Bey, representative of Transjordan.
371–9996. P.3117. No. 27 of 1923. Ras Ajuzah, Kuwait, Persian Gulf. From S.G. Knox to his Commissioner, Baghdad, Mesopotamia, 18 Dec. 1923.
371–9996. P.3117. No. 693–S of 1923. British Residency and Consulate. Gen. Bushire to Duke of Devonshire, Secretary of State for the Colonies, 18 Dec. 1923.
371–9996. P.3117. Paraphrase telegram from Col. Knox to Secretary of State for the Colonies, 24 Dec. 1923.
71–9996. P.3117. No. 62687 – 1923. Paraphrase telegram from Secretary of State for the Colonies to Col. Knox, Kuwait, 29 Dec. 1923.
371–9996. P.3117. Paraphrase telegram from Col. Knox, Kuwait, to Secretary of State for the Colonies, 29 Dec. 1923.
371–9996. P.3117. Paraphrase telegram from Secretary of State to High Commissioner for Iraq, 30 Dec. 1923.
371–9996. P.3117. No. 4. Paraphrase telegram from High Commissioner for Iraq to Secretary of State for the Colonies, 3 Jan. 1924.

371-9996. P.3117. Paraphrase telegram from Col. Knox, Kuwait, to Secretary of State for the Colonies, 6 Jan. 1924.
371-9996. P.3117. No. 1078-24. Paraphrase telegram from Secretary of State for the Colonies to Col. Knox, Kuwait.
371-9996. P.3117. Copy E860-4-91. Communicated by Colonial Office, 22 Jan. Extract from Intelligence Report No. 1. Baghdad, 10 Jan. 1924.
371-9996. P.3117. Paraphrase telegram from Col. Knox, Kuwait, to Secretary of State for the Colonies, 11 Jan. 1924.
371-9996. P.3117. No. 1535-24. Paraphrase telegram from Secretary of State for the Colonies to High Commissioner for Iraq, 14 Jan. 1924.
371-9996. P.3117. Paraphrase telegram from High Commissioner for Iraq to Secretary of State for the Colonies, 15 Jan. 1924.
371-9996. P.3117. No. 85. M.1921. File No. 428. Copy 11-7-1. Trevor, Bushire, to British Agent, Jiddah, 15 Jan. 1924.
371-9996. P.3117. Paraphrase telegram from Col. Knox, Kuwait, to Secretary of State for the Colonies, 17 Jan. 1924.
371-9996. P.3117. No. 2587-1924. Paraphrase telegram from Secretary of State for the Colonies to High Commissioner for Iraq, 18 Jan. 1924.
371-9996. P.3117. No. 2. M.1923. File No. 428, 390. Copy 11-7-1. Foreign Office to British Agent, Jiddah, 18 Jan. 1924.
371-9996. P.3117. British Agent, Jiddah, to Foreign Office, 19 Jan. 1924.
371-9996. P.3117. Paraphrase telegram from High Commissioner for Palestine to Secretary of State for the Colonies, 20 Jan. 1924.
371-9996. P.3117. Paraphrase telegram from Col. Knox, Kuwait, to Secretary of State for the Colonies, 21 Jan. 1924.
371-9996. P.3117. Downing Street. Urgent. No. quoted 2819-24. Under-secretary of State, 22 Jan. 1924.
371-9996. P.3117. Paraphrase telegram from Col. Knox, Kuwait, to Secretary of State for the Colonies, 25 Jan. 1924.
371-9996. P.3117. Copy E812-4-91. 3885-24. Subject: Kuwait Conference. Colonial Office, Downing Street, 25 Jan. 1924.
371-9996. P.3117. Paraphrase telegram, 27 Jan. 1924.
371-9996. P.3117. Paraphrase telegram, 39 Jan. 1924.

BOOKS IN ARABIC

'Abd Rabbihi, al-Sayyid 'Abd al-Hafiz. *Faysal fi Qimmat al-Tarikh*. Cairo: Dar al-Kitab al-Misri, 1977.
'Abd al-Rahim, 'Abd al-Rahim 'Abd al-Rahman. *Al-Dawla al-Sa'udiyya al-Ula*. No pl.: Ma'had al-Buhuth wa'l-Dirasat al-'Arabiyya, 1976.

'Abd al-Rahman, Ibrahim. *Aswad al-Sa'ud wa Tajribati fi'l-Hayah*. Beirut: Dar al-Najah, 1972.

Abu 'Aliya, 'Abd al-Fattah. *Dirasa fi Masadir Tarikh al-Jazira al-'Arabiyya*. Riyadh: Dar al-Marikh, 1979.

———*Al-Dawla al-Sa'udiyya al-Thaniya* AH *1256–1309*. No pl.: Mu'assasat al-Anwar, 1977.

al-'Ajlani, Munir. *Tarikh al-Bilad al-'Arabiyya al-Sa'udiyya*. Beirut: Dar al-Kitab al-'Arabi, n.d.

Amishan, Banu. *'Abd al-'Aziz al-Sa'ud. Sirat Batal wa Mawlid Mamlaka*. Trans. 'Abd al-Fattah Yasin. Beirut: Dar al-Kitab al-'Arabi, n.d.

'Anan, Muhammad. *Al-Sa'udiyya wa Humum al-'Arab khilal Nisf Qarn 1923–1978*. Beirut: al-Maktab al-'Alami, n.d.

al-'Aqqad, 'Abbas Mahmud. *Ma'a 'Ahil al-Jazira al-'Arabiyya*. Beirut: al-Maktaba al-'Asriyya, n.d.

'Assa, Ahmad. *Mu'jiza fawq al-Rimal*. No pl.: no pub., n.d.

Al-Atlas al-Tarikhi li'l-Dawla al-Sa'udiyya. No pl.: Darat al-Malik 'Abd al-'Aziz, 1972.

'Attar, Ahmad 'Abd al-Ghafur. *Saqr al-Jazira*. Jiddah: Matabi' al-Mu'assasa al-'Arabiyya, AH 1384.

al-Badiwi, Muhammad Ahmad. *Al-Mutawakkil 'ala al-Wudud 'Abd al-'Aziz al-Sa'ud*. Riyadh: no pub., 1977.

Bankar, K.M. *Asiya wa'l-Saytara al-Gharbiyya*. Trans. 'Abd al-'Aziz Tawfiq Jawid. No pl.: Dar al-Ma'arif, n.d.

al-Biladi, 'Atiq. *Mu'jam Ma'alim al-Hijaz*. Mecca: Mu'assasat Mecca, 1978.

al-Bustani, Wadi'. *Nabdha Tarikhiyya 'an Najd*. Dictated by Prince Dari b. Fahid al-Rashid AH 1331. Riyadh: Dar al-Yamama, 1966.

al-Daraji, 'Abd al-Razzaq. *Ja'far Abu'l-Thaman wa Dawruhu fi'l-Haraka al-Wataniyya fi'l-'Iraq 1908–1945*. Baghdad: Dar al-Rashid, n.d.

Darwish, Madiha. *Tarikh al-Dawla al-Sa'udiyya hatta al-Rub' al-Awwal min al-Qarn al-'Ishrin*. Jiddah: Dar al-Shuruq, 1980.

———'Al-'Alaqat al-Sa'udiyya al-Misriyya 1924–1936'. Unpub. PhD dissertation, 1978.

al-Faraj, Khalid Muhammad. *Ahsan al-Qisas*. Cairo: Dar al-Ma'arif, 1971.

Fayid, Mustafa Kamal. *Tarjimat al-Dhikra al-'Arabiyya al-Dhahabiyya*. No pl.: no pub., n.d.

Hallaq, Hassan 'Ali. *Mawqif al-Dawla al-'Uthmaniyya min al-Haraka al-Sahiyuniyya*. Beirut: no pub., 1978.

Hamza, Fu'ad. *Qalb Jazirat al-'Arab*. Riyadh: Maktabat al-Nasr al-Haditha, 1968.

Husayn, Ahmad. *Walid wa ma Walad*. Beirut: al-Maktaba al-'Asriyya, 1975.

Ibn Bashr, 'Uthman 'Abd Allah. *'Unwan al-Majd fi Tarikh Najd.* Riyadh: Matba'at al-Qasim, AH 1385.

Ibn Ghannam, Husayn. *Tarikh Najd.* No pl.: Matba'at al-Madani, AH 1381.

Ibn Khamis, 'Abd Allah b. Muhammad. *Al-Majaz bayna al-Yamama wa al-Hijaz. Nusus wa Abhath Jughrafiyya wa Tarikhiyya 'an Jazirat al-'Arab.* Riyadh: Dar al-Yamama, 1970.

Ibrahim, Sayyid. *Tarikh al-Mamlaka al-'Arabiyya al-Sa'udiyya.* Riyadh: Maktabat al-Riyadh al-Hadith, 1973.

al-Jasir, Hamad. *Madinat al-Riyadh 'abra Atwar al-Tarikh. Nusus wa Abhath Jughrafiyya wa Tarikhiyya 'an Jazirat al-'Arab.* Riyadh: Dar al-Yamama, AH 1386.

Khaduri, Muhammad. *Asbab al-Ihtilal al-Britani li'l-'Iraq.* Mosul: no pub., 1933.

al-Khattab, Raja' Husayn Husayni. *Al-'Iraq bayna 1921–1928. Dirasa fi Tatawwur al-'Alaqat al-'Iraqiyya al-Britaniyya wa Atharaha fi Tatawwur al-'Iraq al-Siyasi.* Najaf: Matba'at al-Nu'man, 1976.

al-Khawli, Hasan Sabri. *Siyasat al-Isti'mar al-Sahiyuniyya tujaha Falastin fi'l-Nisf al-Awwal min al-Qarn al-'Ishrin.* Cairo: Dar al-Ma'arif, 1973.

Khaz'al, Husayn Khalaf. *Tarikh al-Jazira al-'Arabiyya fi 'Asr al-Shaykh Muhammad b. 'Abd al-Wahhab.* Beirut: Dar al-Kitab al-Lubnani, 1982.

Muhammad, Muhammad Awad. *Al-Isti'mar wa'l-Madhahib al-Isti'mariyya.* Cairo: Dar al-Kitab al-'Arabi, 1956.

al-Mukhtar, Salah al-Din. *Tarikh al-Mamlaka al-'Arabiyya al-Sa'udiyya.* Beirut: Dar Maktabat al-Hayah, 1982.

al-Nadawi, Muhammad Isma'il. *Tarikh al-Silat bayna al-Hind wa'l-Bilad al-'Arabiyya.* No pl.: no pub., n.d.

Nawfal, Sayyid. *Al-Khalij al-'Arabi.* Beirut: Dar al-Tali'a, 1969.

Qadri, Ahmad. *Mudhakkirati 'an al-Thawra al-'Arabiyya al-Kubra.* Damascus: no pub., 1956.

Qasimiyya, Khayriyya. *Al-Hukuma al-'Arabiyya fi Dimashq.* Cairo: Dar al-Ma'arif, 1971.

Rafa't, Muhammad. *Asad al-Jazira al-'Arabiyya qala li.* No pl.: no pub., n.d.

Rafiq, 'Abd al-Karim. *Al-'Arab wa'l-'Uthmaniyyun.* Damascus: Maktabat Atlas, 1974.

Rajab, 'Umar al-Faruq. *Dirasat fi Jughrafiyat al-Mamlaka al-'Arabiyya al-Sa'udiyya.* Jiddah: Dar al-Shuruq, 1978.

———*Al-Hijaz. Al-Mintaqa al-Gharbiyya min al-Mamlaka al-'Arabiyya al-Sa'udiyya Arduha wa Sukkanuha. Dirasa Ikulujiyya.* Beirut: Dar al-Shuruq, 1979.

al-Rihani, Amin. *Muluk al-'Arab*. Beirut: no pub., 1923.

Sa'id, Amin. *Tarikh al-Dawla al-Sa'udiyya*. Vol. 1: *Min Muhammad b. Sa'ud ila 'Abd al-Rahman al-Faysal*. Beirut: Dar al-Kitab al-'Arabi, n.d.

Salim, al-Sayyid Mustafa. *Takwin al-Yaman al-Hadith. Al-Yaman wa'l-Imam Yahya 1904–1948*. Cairo: Maktabat Sa'id Ra'fat, 1971.

al-Sayyid al-Raqid, Muhammad 'Abd al-Mun'im. *Al-Ghazuw al-'Uthmani li Misr*. Cairo: no pub., 1972.

al-Shamlan, Sayf. *Min Tarikh al-Kuwayt*. Cairo: Matba'at Nahdat Misr, 1959.

Taha, Jad. *Siyasat Britaniya fi Junub al-Yaman*. No pl.: Dar al-Fikr al-'Arabi, 1970.

Tarikh al-Bilad. Based on *Lam' al-Shihab fi Sirat Muhammad b. 'Abd al-Wahhab*. By either an unknown writer or Hasan al-Rabki.

Wahba, Hafiz. *Khamsun 'Aman fi Jazirat al-'Arab*. Cairo: Maktabat wa Matba'at Mustafa al-Babi al-Halabi, 1960.

al-Zamil, 'Abd Allah al-'Ali. *Asdaq al-Bunud fi Tarikh 'Abd al-'Aziz al-Sa'ud*. Beirut: al-Mu'assasa al-Tijariyya, 1972.

al-Zayn, Zayn. *Nushu' al-Qawmiyya al-'Arabiyya*. Beirut: no pub., 1968.

al-Zirikli, Khayr al-Din. *Shibh al-Jazira fi 'Ahd al-Malik 'Abd al-'Aziz*. Beirut: Dar al-'Ilm li'l-Malayin, 1977.

———*Al-Wajiz fi Sirat al-Malik 'Abd al-'Aziz*. Beirut: Dar al-'Ilm li'l-Malayin, 1972.

BOOKS IN ENGLISH

Almana, Mohammed. *Arabia Unified. A Portrait of Ibn Saud*. London: Hutchinson, 1980.

Blunt, Lady Anne. *A Pilgrimage to Nejd*. London: John Murray, 1881. (Reprint: London, Darf, 1984).

Brockelmann, Carl (ed.). *History of the Islamic People*. London: Routledge & Kegan Paul, 1948.

Holt, P.M. *Egypt and the Fertile Crescent 1516–1922*. London: no pub. 1966.

Ireland, W. *Iraq*. No pl.: no pub., n.d.

Lybyer, Albert. *The Turkish Parliament*. No pl.: no pub., n.d.

Ramsaur. *The Young Turks: Prelude to the Revolution of 1908*. USA: no pub., n.d.

Shave, E.K. *History of the Ottoman Empire and Modern Turkey*. No pl.: no pub., n.d.

Troeller, Gary. *The Birth of Saudi Arabia. Britain and the Rise of the House of Sa'ud*. London: Frank Cass, 1976.
Vucinich, S. *The Ottoman Empire. Its Records and Legacy*. No pl.: no pub., 1965.
Wahba, Sheikh Hafiz. *Arabian Days*. London: Arthur Barker, 1964.

Index

Index